Especially for

....

From

....

Date

....

Member of the
Evangelical Christian
Publishers Association

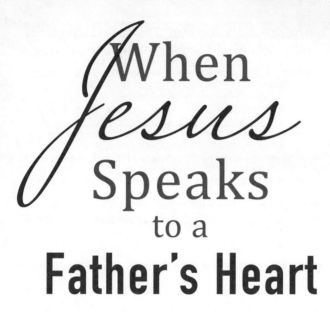

When *Jesus* Speaks to a Father's Heart

David McLaughlan

A Devotional Journal

BARBOUR BOOKS
An Imprint of Barbour Publishing, Inc.

HELP WITH THE HARVEST

Then he said to his disciples, "The harvest is plentiful
but the workers are few. Ask the Lord of the harvest,
therefore, to send out workers into his harvest field."
MATTHEW 9:37–38 NIV

———————◆———————

As a rule, I would never suggest anything that takes you away from your family, but there's a lot of good work that needs doing out there.

"Why me?" you ask. "What difference could one man make? Wouldn't it be better if I focused on my family?" Good questions, and I'm glad you asked them.

I'm asking you because you are at the center of My attention. Though working to bring in My harvest might take you away from your family for a time, what you have to offer might be just the thing someone you haven't yet met needs. And who's to say you can't find a project to help with in your own community—or one your whole family can help with?

If it's not possible to get your family involved, consider the effect seeing their father voluntarily putting his interests aside to help others has on your children. In that scenario, even your absence would be an inspiration.

Then, before you know it, a new crop of helpers—inspired by your example—will soon be helping with the harvest.

———————◆———————

Heavenly Father, thank You for choosing me to help with Your harvest.
Help me to use my talents to strengthen Your kingdom and encourage
new workers to the task. May the work of Your kingdom
be the good soil that encourages my family to grow. Amen.

PLACE THE NAME

"But everyone who denies me here on earth,
I will also deny before my Father in heaven."
MATTHEW 10:33 NLT

A dmit it—there are places you feel comfortable using My name and places you don't. At church or among friends who share the faith, My name will be a regular part of the conversation. But at work, or when you're out with friends who aren't in the faith. . .then My name is mentioned less—or not at all.

Who taught you to be embarrassed like that? And what can you do about it? That is just the way of the world, but not the way it has to be for you.

Imagine your children hearing you make a business arrangement including the words "Lord willing," hearing you end a prayer in a restaurant with "in Jesus' name," or seeing you help a stranger and saying, "God bless you!"

Then they would grow up believing My name belongs in all those places. You would be sparing them the awkwardness with which the enemy usually fills those moments. And you will move a little closer to Me each time you do it. And you just might help someone your embarrassment might previously have kept you from reaching.

Lord God, there is glory, honor, power, and majesty in Your holy name. Help me to use it every day in different situations. Guide me on how best to place You before those who most need the introduction. Empower me with Your Holy Spirit to be bold in speaking Your name. Amen.

NO "LEAST" INVOLVED

"And the King will say, 'I tell you the truth, when you did it to one of the least of these my brothers and sisters, you were doing it to me!' "
MATTHEW 25:40 NLT

———◆———

The guy who pays your salary or the guy who delivers your mail. . .the ex-athlete who coaches the local team or the custodian who takes care of the sports ground—which are you most likely to meet up with or invite to dinner?

It's a hypothetical situation, I know. But think about it. Can you see a possible divide there?

If you set the example for your children, consciously or not, that one "level" of people is more deserving of your time than another, if you raise them to feel more at home in a certain social strata—then how are they ever going to find, let alone help, "the least of these"?

When I ask people to meet Me, it isn't for a flying visit and a quick return to what I was doing before. When that happens, people know they are being condescended to. What really helps them is when My followers are comfortable enough—and care enough—to sit awhile.

Teach your children, by your example, that there are no different levels of humanity. There is only Me—and those I love.

———◆———

Gracious God, I am made in Your image, as is every person I meet.
How can I convince them of that if I do not first convince myself?
Help me love the way You love, without prejudice
or judgment. In Jesus' name, amen.

A SHEPHERD OF THEIR FAITH

Watch your life and doctrine closely. Persevere in them,
because if you do, you will save both yourself and your hearers.
1 TIMOTHY 4:16 NIV

———————————◆———————————

A s head of the household, you have a lot in common with a shepherd: you keep everyone safe, sheltered, and fed. And I know you want to do a good job.

But there's something you may be overlooking. I need you to be a shepherd of your children's faith. Now, that doesn't mean giving them a bunch of heavy-handed "Thou-shalt-nots." It means knowing that there are lots of half-truths and fictions out there that might cause your young lambs to stray, and it means protecting them from those deceptions.

I'm not suggesting you lock your children away and only let them out of the house for church. I'm suggesting you take an active interest in *their* interests. Discuss their interests with them and explore the possibilities. And always have a better option.

How do you do that? You start by reading My Word. No matter how wonderful the latest philosophy may sound, the Bible always has the better alternative.

You might not have a crook for this part of your shepherding duties, but My Word will always provide you with a rod and a staff.

———————————◆———————————

Lord, as the God who is also our Shepherd, You would never leave one
sheep behind. May I have even a fraction of that wonderful, undeserved
love in my heart so that, following in Your steps, I may guide all my
little sheep, and even a few strays, to Your heavenly fold. Amen.

I KNOW A GUY WHO KNOWS

If you need wisdom, ask our generous God, and he will
give it to you. He will not rebuke you for asking.
JAMES 1:5 NLT

———————◆———————

Being head of the family is a big responsibility. For one thing, your children look to you as the ultimate source of wisdom and authority for living their earthly lives.

Now, you and I know that you won't have all the answers. Sometimes Mom might be expected to know everything, but. . .

Being asked questions you can't answer and being expected to deal with situations in which you don't have a clue for what to do can lead to a lot of frustration. So, don't try to do it yourself. Don't set yourself up so that your children expect you to know all the answers. And don't be afraid to say, "Let's ask God."

Your children will still respect and love you. Between you and Me, you will be a wiser man for turning to the Father, who really does know everything and really can handle every situation.

More than that, you will be steering your children away from the future heartache of thinking they have to handle everything on their own. If they see that Dad is okay with saying, "I don't know—but I'm sure God does," they'll be okay with that too.

———————◆———————

Father God, as our all-knowing Creator, there is no greater or
higher authority than You. May I always turn to You for guidance,
setting that good and godly example for my children to follow. Amen.

I BELONG TO. . .

Through him we received grace and apostleship to call all the Gentiles
to the obedience that comes from faith for his name's sake. And you also
are among those Gentiles who are called to belong to Jesus Christ.
ROMANS 1:5–6 NIV

———————◆———————

Have you seen the guy wearing the T-shirt that says *Property of. . .* and then there's the name of his favorite bar? Or the guy who "worships" his football team with a passion shown nowhere else in his life?

I love these people dearly, and I can take a joke. But there's a good chance they have their priorities mixed up. Why am I being such a killjoy? Because the devil has set a lot of traps out there, and I want you to do everything you can to avoid them.

Enjoy your life, by all means. But if you are the "property of" something other than the Father, if you worship more enthusiastically at the football stadium than you do at church, you are showing your children how to make your own idol, your own "golden calf."

If your children witness that, how can you expect them to make Me their priority?

Wear the funny T-shirt and have a great time at the game—or on the lake, or at the races—but while you do these things, make sure it's obvious to everyone whose "property" you really are.

———————◆———————

Guard my heart, O Lord, from any kind of idol worship.
Focus my mind on what is true and good. For only
You are worthy of praise and adoration. Amen.

LITTLE TRUTHS

Jesus said to the people who believed in him, "You are truly my disciples if you remain faithful to my teachings. And you will know the truth, and the truth will set you free."
JOHN 8:31–32 NLT

———————◆———————

I smiled when Mark Twain said, "If you tell the truth, you don't have to remember anything."

When I said, "You shall know the truth and the truth shall set you free," I was talking on a universal scale. But it also sets you free from the little things of life like—as Mr. Twain noted—having to remember which lie you told.

Each lie comes with a cost. It might be a nagging guilty feeling, the fear of being found out, a little lessening of your self-worth, or the inevitable punishment. But young minds don't always comprehend that.

Make it a point to speak to your children about the importance of always telling the truth. Teach them that no matter how attractive the alternative might seem, telling the truth really is the best, easiest (in the long term), and most life-affirming way. Even talk to them of the temptations to be untruthful you have overcome, and what the advantages of being truthful were for you.

If you know you haven't gotten to that point yet yourself, then practice it so you can preach it.

Remember, all those little truths eventually lead to the universal Truth: Me.

———————◆———————

Father, Your truth has set me free. Open my lips to pass that truth to my children. May my actions always reflect Your words and always show Your truth to the next generation of disciples. Amen.

ALWAYS THE PROTECTOR

The LORD is my rock, my fortress, and my savior; my
God is my rock, in whom I find protection. He is my shield,
the power that saves me, and my place of safety.
PSALM 18:2 NLT

Many and varied are the roles a father plays in his child's life. You are the provider, the encourager, the chief source of discipline, teacher, and friend. But above all, you must be the protector.

It's a lot to ask, and it can seem overwhelming at times. But I've seen your heart, and I know it is capable of that and more. And in return, I will be all of those things for you.

Don't be afraid to let your children know where your strength comes from, who tops off your courage when you need it, who teaches you how to be the man you were made to be, and who walks beside you when it seems no one else can.

Then, when your days on earth are done and the good in you is weighed against the other stuff, and you can't help but wonder what judgment will hold for you, I'll be right there, speaking up for you—your Protector to the end.

Until I do that for you, you do it for your children. I'm telling you, it'll make My job a whole lot easier.

My Protector and Savior, I feel so weak at times. I am grateful
that You know the man I can be. Help me be a strong tower
for those You have placed in my care. Amen.

HELP TO THE HELPLESS

*Religion that God our Father accepts as pure and faultless
is this: to look after orphans and widows in their distress
and to keep oneself from being polluted by the world.*
JAMES 1:27 NIV

Back in New Testament times, widows and orphans were the most vulnerable people in society. If I (or the apostle James) wanted examples to stress the importance of helping the helpless, they were the obvious candidates.

The same might not always be true today. The widows and orphans in your locality might be well taken care of. But there will always be someone filling the role of the neediest. All you have to do is look around and seek them out.

But while I'm on the subject, the widows and orphans who live near you—whatever else they may have, they don't have what your family has: a man to do the man stuff, someone to be a dad every now and again.

Now I know you have your own responsibilities, and you can't be everything to everyone. But you can still help. You might even see it as a way of giving thanks for the privilege of being your wife's husband and your child's father.

What's that? You don't have the time or the energy? Well, that would probably make you one of the needy. And I can help you there, too.

---

*Light of the world, shine Your guiding light in the dark places of
my life, the wasted time and the lost hours. Turn them toward
Your work that I might better meet others' needs. In Your name, amen.*

DAD ON DUTY

"Appoint the residents of Jerusalem to act as guards, everyone on a regular watch. Some will serve at sentry posts and some in front of their own homes."
NEHEMIAH 7:3 NLT

Does being a dad ever seem like too much to bear? Does it ever feel as if it's you against the world?

Before you answer, remember how well I know your heart.

So let me take you to the military for encouragement. When soldiers camp for the night, they don't assign one man to stand guard over the campsite all night long. Each man stands a four-hour watch, and usually another sentry stands guard with him. The two of them keep the camp safe until the next watch arrives.

You aren't the first father by a long, long way. Many men have done the work, have dealt with the frustrations, and have successfully carried out their duty as fathers, and many more will follow. Your job isn't to win the whole fatherhood "war," although it seems like it at times. You just need to stand a watch. You can do that, can't you?

If you need a little moral support, there are other guys out there on duty, too. And, of course, I am always willing to stand the watch with you.

Father, I thank You that I have Your armor to protect me. May Your shield of faith, helmet of salvation, and sword of the Spirit empower me as I stand guard over my family.
In Jesus' name I pray, amen.

WELCOME TO MY WORLD

He was with God in the beginning. Through him all things
were made; without him nothing was made that has been made.
JOHN 1:2–3 NIV

Would it sadden you to know that most of the things you do as a
father will go unnoticed—or soon be forgotten? Well, it shouldn't.

Think back to your own childhood. Do you remember every lift, kiss,
and hug? Can you recall the things your dad did around the house to
make it safer and more comfortable for you? How many gifts were you
given in love, and how few of them do you now recall?

The memory of the things you do for your children will be just as
transient as those of the things your father did for you, but the overall
effect of those things will be an environment where your children can
thrive.

Imagine being Me. Everything—and I mean *everything*—was
made through Me. But look around you and see how little that work is
appreciated.

If We had the chance to do it again, would We do it differently,
just because We knew the appreciation would be less than We deserve?
Or would We keep doing far more for our children than they will ever
know?

I choose the latter. Will you?

God, the Author and Creator of all, I look around me and often don't
see the wonders of Your world—or even appreciate my amazing family.
May I take time each day to revel in at least one of Your marvelous works,
thank You for it, and then share my gratitude with others. Amen.

PERFECTLY IMPERFECT

*"He is the Rock; his deeds are perfect. Everything he does is just and fair.
He is a faithful God who does no wrong; how just and upright he is!"*
DEUTERONOMY 32:4 NLT

B race yourself for this, but there hasn't been an earthly father yet who didn't let his children down at some point.

I love the way you bridled at the thought that you might have at some time disappointed your children. Perfect people wouldn't let their children down, but your reaction to the possibility that you may have is more than perfect. It's wonderful!

You are trying to overcome an innately flawed nature by filling the cracks with love. And that's how you draw closer to the Father who never let anyone down.

On the bright side, your flaws allow space for your children to grow. And your annoyance at not being perfect for them produces growth for you, too.

Of course, if you were perfect, your children would need no one else. Having such a father on earth would remove the need for an all-knowing, all-powerful, all-providing Father in heaven.

So, when you mess up as a father, as you will, get annoyed enough to do it better next time—but don't beat yourself up. You see, when you get right down to it, even your shortcomings are part of the greater plan.

Faithful Lord, give me love, joy, peace, patience, kindness, goodness, faithfulness, gentleness, and self-control when dealing with my children. May the fruits of Your Spirit grow in me that I may show them the power of the perfect Father. Amen.

HEROES REARRANGED

*When Jesus had entered Capernaum, a centurion came
to him, asking for help. "Lord," he said, "my servant
lies at home paralyzed, suffering terribly."*
MATTHEW 8:5–6 NIV

———————◆◆———————

T he things that impress you enough to talk about them will help shape
what your children think is important. Take some time to think
about that.

Are you impressed with movie heroes? Do top athletes or NASCAR
drivers get your admiration? Well, actually, that's fine if you admire or
are impressed with talented and accomplished people.

But what about those who openly display acts of love—those silly,
soft things most "tough" guys just seem unable to do.

Enjoying movies and sports are fine, but make sure you point out to
your children the guy who risks ridicule to show affection, the woman
who does without so her children can have what they need, or the man
who breaks the behavioral habit of a lifetime because someone needs
him to. Make a big deal of them. If you can help others while you do that,
then so much the better.

Love in action takes more courage than doing your own stunts in
a movie. Look out for those moments and help your children see how
wonderful these acts of love really are. Rearrange your list of heroes to
make room for a few people doing My work.

———————◆◆———————

*Lord Jesus, You showed me ultimate heroism by dying for my
sins. Help me to show my family where my priorities lie and the
sacrifices I will willingly make for their salvation. Amen.*

BUILT ON THE ROCK

"Anyone who listens to my teaching and follows it is wise, like a person who builds a house on solid rock."
MATTHEW 7:24 NLT

———◆———

If I were to tell you that you should not simply give your child everything he asks you for, am I being a Scrooge McDuck, or am I just trying to save you some money?

Actually, it's neither of those.

On one level, if your children want something substantial—as in something expensive or requiring a long-term commitment—then you can talk with them about what it involves, what impact it might have, and how best they might go about getting it.

This might sound a little mundane, but it will provide some great teaching opportunities—times you and your children can plan ahead together, times you can encourage them along the road of achievement, and times you can celebrate with them when they get what they wanted.

But, you may be asking, what about the spiritual application of what I've just said? Well, when you take the time to talk to your kids about the things they want, you will also be teaching them to build their values on solid footings and not on their earthly desires. As you instill those kinds of values when it comes to the things they want, you can encourage them to do the same in other areas, too. And what is the most solid of footings? Me!

———◆———

Generous God, Provider of all, help me to lay a firm foundation for my family to build on. May it be fixed firmly in Your Word so that the principles of Christian living will be clear for all who associate with us to see. Amen.

ASK THE EXPERT

Fathers, do not exasperate your children; instead,
bring them up in the training and instruction of the Lord.
EPHESIANS 6:4 NIV

———————◆———————

Y ou know those times when the problems of fatherhood leave you at a loss for what to do? Where do you turn when nothing you say to your children seems to make the situation any better?

Guys are notorious for not asking for help. If you were going to embarrass yourself by asking for advice, it would have to be from a real expert, someone who knows your situation inside and out. And there really isn't anyone who knows everything.

Or is there?

Have you ever heard the term "Our Father"? That "our" encompasses children and relationships beyond counting. There isn't a difficult or awkward situation He hasn't been involved in. And He has the answer for every one of them.

So why are there ever any familial problems? Because stubborn guys like you (and stubborn women and children—but, let's face it, guys are the worst about this) don't ask Him for advice.

You wouldn't try to figure out the computerized systems in your car by yourself; you'd call for an expert. So why should your parenting be any different? It isn't any less complicated. So go on, ask the expert.

———————◆———————

Almighty God, there is nothing You haven't experienced or don't
have complete control over. Remove my pride that I may be
humble before Jehovah-Shalom—my Lord of peace. Amen.

NOT SPECIAL. . .PRECIOUS

Therefore, since we have these promises, dear friends,
let us purify ourselves from everything that contaminates body
and spirit, perfecting holiness out of reverence for God.
2 CORINTHIANS 7:1 NIV

It's a subtle distinction, perhaps, but I don't want you fathers to teach your children that they are *special*. Rather, I want you to raise them knowing they are *precious*.

Teaching your children that they are *special* might lead them to believe they are "different" or that special allowances will be made for them. But teaching them that they are precious lets them know that you value them. When they know how precious they are, they will grow to understand that they are worth more than the many options they will encounter to diminish themselves.

Having talked about how precious your children are, I want to remind you that you are every bit as precious to My (and your) heavenly Father. When you fail to understand that, you will tend to make allowances for yourself. But when you think about how much I value you, then you are less likely to indulge in behaviors and habits that diminish your children's father in their eyes.

Just as the "little gems" can be encouraged to glisten and shine as His children, so you can be like polished gold as His deputy in fatherhood.

Thank You, Lord, for Your generosity. Your presence in my life is more valuable than silver, more precious than gold, and longer lasting than diamonds. I am made in Your image, so help me to be a reflection of You and a good example for my own precious gems. Amen.

AN EASY STEP AWAY

*"Truly I tell you, anyone who will not receive the kingdom
of God like a little child will never enter it."*
LUKE 18:17 NIV

———————◆———————

I told My followers that they had to become as little children for some very important reasons. Be honest. Do you forgive more easily now than you did when you were little? Do you love as honestly, trust as completely, and sleep with as clear a conscience as you did when you were a child?

I know you don't.

But even that purer state of living isn't what I have in store for you and yours when I tell you to be like a little child. But it's closer—*much* closer.

To some degree, you can encourage the good and limit the effects of the bad in your child's life. Most people don't take that responsibility too seriously, but I'm asking you to make it a priority. Help your children preserve what is, after all, their freedom from fear. If they don't need to fear, they won't need to adopt those "protective strategies" that, coincidentally, keep Me out.

Help them live the kind of lives that are only a short, easy step away from heaven.

And if you learn a thing or two about being more childlike in the process, well. . .that would make Me as happy as a two-year-old.

———————◆———————

*My God and King, show me Your kingdom here on this earth. Free me from
the protective strategies I have built up as I have grown to adulthood.
I know these things are cages the enemy has constructed for me.
May I mirror my children in their trust and fearlessness.
In Jesus' name I pray, amen.*

SERVANT ON A MISSION

"For even the Son of Man came not to be served but to serve others and to give his life as a ransom for many."
MATTHEW 20:28 NLT

———◆———

Head of the family? you think. *Yeahhh! Now everyone has to do stuff for me!*

Excuse me while I laugh!

Did you ever think that being a husband and father was kind of like being the boss and that you could just spend your days telling people what to do?

Tell me. Am I a boss? Am I the head of my Father's own family? Yes, I am. But do you remember that time I washed my friends' feet? Or when I prepared lunch for more than five thousand hungry people? Or when I had something to do for you that had Me sweating blood—but I did it anyway?

That's what being the head of a family is all about. It's far different from the world's idea of what a boss is. It's about being a servant first—and sometimes it's no picnic. It's about being the kind of boss I was when I came to earth to serve.

Like Me, the heavenly Father made you the head of your family so you could be a servant—a servant on a mission.

———◆———

Lord, give me a servant's heart. As I diminish, may my willingness to follow and obey You grow. I want to be ready and available to act out Your vision for me and my family. As a willing and obedient man, I bow before my Servant King. Amen.

BEYOND THE BITE

You must each decide in your heart how much to give.
And don't give reluctantly or in response to pressure.
"For God loves a person who gives cheerfully."
2 Corinthians 9:7 NLT

W hat's the point in encouraging children to give to charitable causes? As the parent, you only end up replacing the money. But suppose I suggested that you didn't—replace the money, that is.

You know that feeling of having done a good thing when you help someone out? How different would it feel if someone immediately gave you back the money you just gave away?

So why would you deprive your child of that feeling that comes from doing good for others? Because you don't want them to go without? You wouldn't be. In letting them feel the "bite" of using their own money to help with a cause that means something to them, you also give them the pleasure of knowing they gave of themselves. And that's a habit we in heaven are very fond of.

Of course, if you then find a way to reward them without them knowing it's a reward. . .well. . .you'll be following in a very good tradition. After all, the Father does that for you all the time.

My God and Provider, all I have comes from You. I freely
honor You with my wealth and firstfruits. I will not rob
You of what is Yours. May I teach my children that
giving in Your name is a joyous thing. Amen.

TURN THE THORN AROUND

Therefore, in order to keep me from becoming conceited, I was
given a thorn in my flesh, a messenger of Satan, to torment me.
Three times I pleaded with the Lord to take it away from me.
2 Corinthians 12:7–8 niv

———◆———

L et's address that nagging doubt of yours. You know, the one where
you aren't a good father—or at least not as good as your dad was.

How did I know you felt like that? Because I know that most fathers
feel that way—at least at times. I remember your dad felt the same
when recalling his dad.

But you know what? It's a lie!

So what can you do about it? Well, the apostle Paul provided a
solution when he wrote of a thorn in his side. He never came out and
said what it was, but he said it spurred him on. In his attempts to
overcome this thorn, he did things he might not have if it hadn't been
there.

Satan hates it when we use his own tricks against him. So I'm not
going to tell you you're an amazing dad. Let's leave that thorn of doubt
there. Let its constant prodding urge you to become better and better,
until you are the best father you can be.

———◆———

Lord, protect me from Satan's lies with Your truth. I rejoice
that You are the reverser of all his works, the destroyer
of his schemes, and always the better option. Amen.

EATING TO THRIVE

But Jesus told him, "No! The Scriptures say, 'People do not live by
bread alone, but by every word that comes from the mouth of God.' "
MATTHEW 4:4 NLT

Man shall not live by bread alone—and children shouldn't either. Feeding your children really nutritious food may not be your strong point. You might be more the barbecue or hot dogs kind of guy, but you wouldn't expect your children to thrive on an exclusively takeout or fast-food diet. You also probably wouldn't want them to exist on a diet of only the "foods" they saw advertised on television.

Which brings Me to another kind of diet.

Television, movies, the Internet, advertising. . .if information were food, most children these days would be overfed but malnourished— eating plenty but failing to thrive.

Give them other options. If you have to give up one of your TV subscriptions to do it, then it probably wouldn't be a channel you would share with them anyway. Keep their diet in mind when you choose trips to the movies. Or go the totally old-fashioned route and encourage them to read a good book.

Mom might be the one cooking up the physical food. See if you can't cook up some spiritual nourishment.

Give me a wise and discerning heart, my Savior. May my moral
compass always point unwaveringly in Your direction. Shower
me with spiritual refreshment so I can keep my family safely
on Your path. In Your blessed name, amen.

THE NEXT GENERATION

"So now I give him to the LORD. For his whole life he will be given over to the LORD." And he worshiped the LORD there.
1 SAMUEL 1:28 NIV

———————◆———————

You can train good soldiers. There are techniques that, practiced enough, can make good gymnasts. And there are things that can be taught and learned before a driver-to-be takes the license exam.

Wouldn't it be wonderful if there were a set of exercises you could go through with your child to guarantee that a boy would be a good dad or a girl the kind of mom anyone would be glad to have? I should imagine if that were possible, someone would have written the rule book long ago, and parents these days would be too awesome for words.

I'm going to suggest that you don't bother with all that.

You and your kids' mother aren't here to produce the next generation of moms and dads, so you don't have to worry about making them better at the job than you are. Your only responsibility is to produce the next generation of godly men and women.

Raise your children to be nothing more and nothing less than delights unto the Lord. The Holy Spirit will take care of the rest.

———————◆———————

Majestic Maker of all things, thank You for my unique family. Mold and fill us. Enable us and empower us. Raise us up on wings like eagles so that we may show justice, love mercy, and walk humbly with our God. Amen.

CREATION'S TOUR GUIDE

*Then God looked over all he had made, and he saw
that it was very good! And evening passed and
morning came, marking the sixth day.*
GENESIS 1:31 NLT

———————◆———————

The kingdom of heaven is going to be awesome when it comes! But in the meantime, My own creation is not a bad place to wait. Okay, there's a lot of wrong stuff out there, but it pales in comparison with the good, the beautiful, the kind, the mind-bogglingly complex, the little clues to the greater plan. . .

The Father's work is never less than praiseworthy, and as His deputy here in the world, you get to teach your children to look for it, to expect it, and to delight in it. Share the experience with them and give thanks together for His wonderful work and His unimaginably generous gift.

From the daisy in the grass, to the eagle in the sky, to the surf on the sand, to the sun on your face—thank God for all of it.

As your children's guide through God's amazing work, you will look pretty cool in your children's eyes. And you'll make your own journey through this world more wonderful in doing so.

———————◆———————

*From the rising of the sun to its setting, Your name is to be praised,
my Lord. From the mountaintops to the ocean's depth, Your name is
to be praised. Help me give my children that knowledge and to
share that wonder every time they step outside. Amen.*

NOT A COMPETITION. . .A COOPERATION

As it is, there are many parts, but one body.
The eye cannot say to the hand, "I don't need you!"
And the head cannot say to the feet, "I don't need you!"
1 CORINTHIANS 12:20–21 NIV

———— ◆ ————

You know that guy you're always trying to beat? Okay, there's more than one. There's the one you want to be fitter than, the guy whose job you should be doing, the man who's just better at. . .everything.

People know, and your children will pick up on it. If you don't think you're so hot—and you're the best dad in the world, according to them—then what chance do they have?

Lay it aside. You'll be doing yourself a big favor. These guys aren't your competitors, and you shouldn't be theirs. Appreciate their strengths and value your own. In doing so, you will teach the little ones that life isn't about competition but about cooperation.

I know how that sounds in worldly terms—kind of like you're setting your children up to lose. But since when did I care what the world thought?

I say again, life is not a competition. Those guys you want to outdo are family. They might not realize it yet, but I want you to teach them, and your children, that they are.

———— ◆ ————

Heavenly King, You have chosen me to be part of a royal priesthood
by calling me out of darkness. Keep me walking in the light,
empowering me through the Holy Spirit to bind me in unity
with all Your family members. Amen.

GREAT VICTORIES IN LITTLE WAYS

But He turned and said to Peter, "Get behind Me, Satan!
You are an offense to Me, for you are not mindful of
the things of God, but the things of men."
MATTHEW 16:23 NKJV

———————◆———————

G et behind me, Satan!"
You can't beat an emphatic, heroic declaration that puts the
enemy in his place. But life isn't always that clear-cut.

Children love stories where heroic efforts are made for the best
of reasons, where little ones succeed when grown-ups fail. There are
stories like that in real life, just not that many of them.

Life is more about small decisions and subtle temptations than
it is about epic battles.

By all means read your children heroic tales and enjoy movies with
them in which love overcomes. But also make them aware of the little
skirmishes and the role they can play in them. Make it a fun game,
albeit an important one. Set a heroic example in firmly and resolutely
overcoming your own temptations, and encourage them to do the
same with theirs.

Show them they can win great victories in little ways. And if they
would like a heroic-sounding catch-phrase to shout when defeating
the enemy, they could do worse than borrowing Mine.

———————◆———————

All-knowing God, temptations come in many forms. Open my eyes to them.
Teach me about them that I might teach others. Guard me and guide me.
Lead me not into temptation, and deliver me from evil. Amen.

DO NOT FORSAKE THEM, OH MY DARLINGS

About three in the afternoon Jesus cried out in a loud voice, "Eli, Eli, lema sabachthani?" *(which means "My God, my God, why have you forsaken me?").*
MATTHEW 27:46 NIV

You'll remember Me crying, "Why have You forsaken me?" How do you think I felt right about then? Abandoned? Alone? Yeah. . .and then some.

There was a plan, and that moment of abandonment was very necessary in fulfilling it. God had it under control.

But imagine a child in that same position. He cries out to his father, but he has walked away. It isn't a part of any grand plan; he's walking because he's hurting and can't think of anything else to do. That child isn't being left for a greater good, and he has no idea if his father will ever come back. He might—but it probably doesn't feel like it to the child.

Imagine how much sympathy I have for that child.

Guys who walk away always think they have a good reason. I might be biased, but I almost never agree with them.

Even if it's only for a little while, or only in a limited way, never forsake your child.

All power is Yours, Lord. You never forsake me. Even in Your "weakness," You taught a mighty lesson. Grant me strength never to walk away from Your love, Your work, or Your children. Amen.

LOVE ABOVE ALL THINGS

*Three things will last forever—faith, hope,
and love—and the greatest of these is love.*
1 CORINTHIANS 13:13 NLT

I know the things you think are important in life: getting ahead at work, meeting all those payments each month, not getting too out-of-shape, being able to hold your head up in your community.

But I also know what would knock all of these things right off your list of priorities.

Imagine if all those things went wrong for you. Picture yourself wiped out, shattered, owning nothing, and feeling worthless. Then imagine your child's arms around your neck, cheek to cheek, and the whispered words, "Dad, I love you."

Now tell Me what in the world could feel that wonderful.

That's why the Father wants your love. It's not that He's the dad who already has everything. It's that He knows the value of love and places it ahead of everything else.

Remember that in bad times and good. Nothing will ever mean as much as your children's love. Make sure they know you feel that way. Oh, and send some love to your heavenly Father while you're at it.

Precious Father, thank You that I can begin to know the depth of Your love for me. And I thank You for sending my children as a reminder of that love. Pour Your love into them—exceedingly, abundantly, beyond measure or expectation—that they may honor and glorify You, too. Amen.

LITTLE FISHERS

"Come, follow me," Jesus said, "and I will send you out to fish for people."
Matthew 4:19 NIV

❦

I love that you are saved, and I love that your children will be raised in the faith. But am I content with that?

Yes, very. . .and yet, no, not at all.

Imagine if I had gathered the disciples around Me and they had believed—and it had stopped there. Then you would never have heard of Me.

For the Word to be heard everywhere, each generation must be fishers of men.

Even if your little ones don't become priests or missionaries, I want them to reflect Me. I want people to see them and wish they had what your children have: Me!

Now, you don't teach your children that by insisting they only go to "holy" places and spend time only with "holy" people. You teach them that by reminding them to take Me wherever they go.

From the youngest age, your children will have influence. It might not come to flower until years later, but that's for the Holy Spirit to worry about.

What I want you to do is raise Me some fine examples of fishers of men. And you'll do that best by being one yourself.

❦

Heavenly Father, You have entrusted me with these children.
May they, in their turn, be trusted with Your work, which is greater
than many generations, so that Your Word will be spread across
the world until every ear hears and every knee bends. Amen.

GIVING, BUT NOT TO RECEIVE

All the believers were together and had everything in common.
They sold property and possessions to give to anyone who had need.
ACTS 2:44–45 NIV

———————◆◆———————

The idea of giving without expecting or desiring anything in return goes against human nature in a couple of ways. But, hey, you know I'm always keen to challenge what people see as their "nature."

Children are often seen as naturally selfish, wanting to keep what's theirs, reluctant to share. But that's a learned behavior. It kicks in if they aren't confident enough that their needs will be met, that what they give away will be replaced by something equally fascinating.

As a father, it's your job to provide that kind of security—the security that allows your children's true nature to shine through.

How do you do that? Well, in the same way I've done it for you. If you're honest with yourself, you know you receive far more than you give, but the Father never makes it seem like there's a direct relationship between the two.

So creating that environment for your children is one challenge. And what's the other? It's this: having learned to give, they will be rewarded abundantly. The big challenge is to make sure they don't think of giving as the ultimate selfish thing to do.

———————◆◆———————

God, You have forgiven my sin, and that was Your greatest generosity.
Help me to freely give as I have freely received, both in material
possessions and in Your love. Show me ways to help my children honor
Your giving example. Help us be a family after Your heart. Amen.

A MAN OF PEACE AT HOME

"If someone slaps you on one cheek, offer the other cheek also.
If someone demands your coat, offer your shirt also."
LUKE 6:29 NLT

———◆◆———

P eace isn't exciting or glamorous, and men often think of war as the flowering of their masculinity. But the cost of conflict is just too high, and it's where the devil does his best work.

Now, you have those protective instincts and abilities for a reason, but strength is best displayed in avoiding conflict rather than rushing into it.

Think about it. An obnoxious guy gets in your face and starts abusing you. Which is the more difficult thing to do, turn the other cheek—or floor him? Now ask yourself how you want your children to behave in times of conflict. You don't want that for them, and I don't want it for you.

Teaching peace isn't easy, which is why we need to start when your children are young. That is why I need you to pay special attention to it.

Be the resolver in your children's conflicts. Show them that with a little effort, both sides can be better off. Then teach them to appreciate the resultant, unexciting, unglamorous, but parent-pleasing peace that results.

———◆◆———

Jehovah Shalom, God of peace, You promised to bless the peacemakers and that they would be children of God. I trust in Your Word and endeavor to be worthy of that promise. Bless my household, restore peace, and reign over us—now and forever. Amen.

THE TRICK OF TEMPTATION

*"Watch and pray so that you will not fall into temptation.
The spirit is willing, but the flesh is weak."*
MATTHEW 26:41 NIV

———◆———

H ow would you feel if someone led your child into temptation? Angry,
I'm sure. But would you be offended if I suggested some of your
behaviors might do that?

Before we get off the topic of temptation, I am going to suggest that
you talk to your children about it. A bit heavy of a subject for children?
Well, yes and no. Temptation does a lot of damage in this world, but
usually through people who aren't prepared for it. So it's important
that you communicate with your children on the subject.

Teach your children to expect temptation. Tell them that the guy
who tempts them by making promises doesn't have the power to deliver
but that God does. Tell them that the guy who makes these promises is
already a busted flush, intent only on doing as much damage as he can
on the way down.

If you do that, they'll be prepared when they have to face temptation
on their own. Then instead of falling into the devil's traps, they will be
more likely to mutter "loser" and laugh as they walk on by to a much
greater reward.

———◆———

*Jesus, You stayed firm in Your resolve when You were tempted for
forty days and nights. Thank You for setting for me that example of
the enemy's ultimate futility. Thank You that I can use it to help
my children make good choices. Praise You, Lord. Amen.*

ETERNAL INSTRUCTION

All Scripture is inspired by God and is useful to teach us what is true and to make us realize what is wrong in our lives. It corrects us when we are wrong and teaches us to do what is right.

2 TIMOTHY 3:16 NLT

Your world changed when you became a father—but the world didn't change.

Lots of things change from generation to generation, but the forces that govern the world remain the same. The truths and values that were best for previous generations still apply. Now that you're a man with responsibilities, it's all the more important you know what they are.

You can ask your elders. But wouldn't it be nice to have them all written down for you?

You know where I am going with this, and, of course, you would expect Me to promote My own book. But ask yourself this: how many generations are there in two thousand years? And why did each of them pass the Bible on to the next—through times of peace and times of trouble?

Because it worked for them. And it will work for you.

As a father, you need to know these truths. Just like your father did. And his father. And his father. Which is why the Father of them all had them written down.

Thank You, Lord, that Your Word is unchanging yet living for me today. Help me use it daily to guide my children. Thank You for the power and instruction in Your eternal Word. Amen.

THE THINGS YOU CAN'T FIX

Wait for the LORD; be strong and take heart and wait for the LORD.
PSALM 27:14 NIV

———◆———

Have you ever heard a woman say, "Men always want to fix things"—as if that were a bad thing?

Men do have a strong bent toward fixing things, and that urge only gets stronger when they become fathers.

Ironically, that's usually when they discover the things they can't fix.

I hate to tell you this, but women have it right in this instance. Not everything *can* be fixed—or should I say, not everything can be fixed *by men*.

You will do plenty of good in your child's life, but sooner or later you will reach a point where all your best efforts achieve nothing. It might even seem like the bridge between you and your child has become irreparably broken. In frustration, the guy who is used to fixing everything might burn whatever remains of that bridge.

Don't be that guy! Be the guy with two extra tools in his toolbox—patience and faith.

If you can't fix it, then that's because God has someone or something else in mind.

———◆———

Dear Lord, I am not the solution to every situation, nor the answer to every question. Remind me that I need only to accept this and turn away from my efforts to fix things—and then allow You to fill the need. I am Your workman when You need me to be, Your humble observer and admirer for all the many times You don't. Amen.

HOW SHALL WE PRAY?

Once Jesus was in a certain place praying. As he finished,
one of his disciples came to him and said, "Lord, teach
us to pray, just as John taught his disciples."
LUKE 11:1 NLT

———————◆———————

Prayer might seem a lot less formal these days, but then it wasn't always formal. Early prayers were often just men shouting from hilltops.

You will play a big role in teaching your children how to talk to their God. When I was asked how it should be done, I taught what has come to be known as the Lord's Prayer. Feel free to use it. There is no copyright. I collect no royalties.

If you want to teach a more formal—or less formal—way to pray, you won't get any objections from heaven. We are particularly fond of the casual, intimate chat that indicates a close, loving relationship.

But there is something I must stress: your children, whether they are asking God for something or thanking Him, will be talking to the One who created the universe.

You can describe it as humility or as great wisdom, but impress on them the importance of including five little words in all their conversations with God: "Your will be done. Amen!"

———————◆———————

Father in heaven, thank You for the template of the Lord's Prayer.
Guide me as I share prayers with my children. Faithful Father,
thank You for all the answered prayers—and for the patience
learned through unanswered prayers.
Your will be done. Amen.

THE HIGHEST STANDARD

Instead, we will speak the truth in love, growing in every way more and more like Christ, who is the head of his body, the church.
EPHESIANS 4:15 NLT

There's no avoiding it—a father is a son's example of what a man ought to be and a daughter's image of what a good husband looks like.

There comes a time when Dad isn't the main man in his children's life anymore. That's difficult for a father to deal with. But his influence and example go on. And that can be even more difficult to deal with.

Every loving father hopes for the best for his children. But I'm here to tell you that you need to do more than hope. You need to set the standard.

It's a universal theme. God wants exactly the same for you. He has big expectations. You are, after all, His handiwork, and He knows what you are capable of.

So did He set a standard for you? Sure He did. He sent Me.

An impossible standard? Well, what have you got to lose by trying?

Be the man you ought to be—for your sake, for your children's sake, and for My sake.

My guiding light and perfect example, all things are possible through and with You. I believe that with the help of the Holy Spirit I can be the man You mean me to be. I step toward this goal in faith and love. Amen.

WAITING IN THE STORM

"And if he finds it, truly I tell you, he is happier about that one
sheep than about the ninety-nine that did not wander off."
MATTHEW 18:13 NIV

———————◆————————

L et's go to the movies!

I'm thinking in particular of *The Day After Tomorrow*. In that film, Dennis Quaid's character is hundreds of miles away when a global storm threatens his son's safety. "Stay where you are," he says. "I'm coming for you!" The son stays put and the father keeps his word. Very reminiscent of the shepherd who sees his ninety-nine sheep to safety and then goes out into a storm for that one last lost lamb.

Now, you might not be a movie star, but you can inspire that kind of trust in your children. It might take a lifetime, and it might never be needed, but I want them to feel that way about you.

I hear you think, *Yeah, that'd be nice, but I couldn't actually be that kind of hero.*

Not on your own maybe. But if you stick by Me, you will have a companion who is used to braving storms. And should you wander and get lost along the way, just stay where you are and know that I'm coming for you.

———————◆————————

Father, help me to be there for Little League, birthdays, dentist appointments, and pediatrician visits. Help me be trustworthy in the small things so my children will trust me in more serious, matters—as I do with You, my Lord and Good Shepherd. Amen.

THE APPLE DOESN'T FALL FAR

"A good tree can't produce bad fruit,
and a bad tree can't produce good fruit."
MATTHEW 7:18 NLT

———— ◆ ————

You don't get apples from a pear tree, and you don't get pears from an apple tree.

Your children should know from an early age that they represent Mom and you. How they behave when you aren't there speaks volumes to the world about the kind of parents you are.

Which doesn't mean you should come on all heavy-handed about it. Tell them what godly behavior looks like, assure them it's a good thing, and then trust them. I think if you could see what they do with that trust, you would be well pleased—at least most of the time.

Of course, it's the other times that cause all the problems. What do you do then? Well, there may or may not be some external factor you can change that would make a difference. But one option is always available: take a look at the tree that produces such troublesome fruit.

Can you be a better example? What would it take for you to be the tree that produces children you would happily think of as the apple of your eye?

———— ◆ ————

Father God, You are the all-supplying Vine and I am a humble branch.
I will remain with You always, ever dependent and thankful. Help me
set my children the best example I can so that my life might
bear fruit that is pleasing to You. In Jesus' name, amen.

REFINE YOUR WORLD

He will sit like a refiner of silver, burning away the dross.
He will purify the Levites, refining them like gold and silver, so that
they may once again offer acceptable sacrifices to the LORD.
MALACHI 3:3 NLT

———————————◆———————————

As a man living in an imperfect world, you hear and see a lot of things—some of them offensive, some thoughtless, and many that break My heart.

You can't help but take it in, and eventually it weighs on your soul.

So what do you do? Do you ease the burden by talking about it to your wife and children? Do you let it change you? Do you allow it to cause you to behave differently with your family?

Psychologists might not agree with Me here, but I am going to recommend a third option: draw strength from love, confident in the knowledge that I am working with you on it, and become like a purifying fire. Burn it up in good works, fixing it where you can and counteracting it when you can't by producing more good.

As a man, you can't control what the world throws at you. But as a father with responsibilities, you get to decide what you do with it. Purify!

———————————◆———————————

Purify my heart, O living Lord. My desire is to be holy, and if my life must pass through the fire, I take it as a blessing, knowing that, freed of impurities, I might become an acceptable offering for You. Amen.

THE HONOR OF RAISING GODLY CHILDREN

*But grow in the grace and knowledge of our Lord and
Savior Jesus Christ. To him be glory both now and forever! Amen.*
2 PETER 3:18 NIV

———◆———

The first few years of any child's life are amazing, aren't they? First there's the fact that they exist at all, and then you wonder as their little personalities begin to develop. Then you go on a journey with them as they explore their world and their own capabilities.

Where does all that go? Perhaps you start to lose the fascination when you are busy at work and they are busy at school. But the development doesn't stop, and the sense of wonder shouldn't, either.

Nothing in this world will grow, change, and develop in so many wonderful ways as your children. Don't let the busyness of the world distract you from that, and don't stop letting them know how much their growth amazes you.

God made your children and filled them with potential. By encouraging them to stay close to Him, you can help make sure they become everything He meant them to be. Rasing your children is meant to be an honor and a treat.

But don't forget He made you the same way. As you watch them grow. . .grow!

———◆———

*Lord, help me find pause in this busy life to truly appreciate
my children. Thank You for giving me the honor of being
their father. Enhance the time I spend with them.
Help me to use it wisely. Amen.*

HIS WONDERS TO PERFORM

Truly, O God of Israel, our Savior,
you work in mysterious ways.
Isaiah 45:15 nlt

———————◆———————

D o you think it's a coincidence that there are more male magicians than female ones in the entertainment industry? Or is it just that men are more interested in making amazing things happen and keener on pulling stuff out of a hat?

Would it be better if faith worked like that? Or would that demean the process?

What I am saying is that to teach your children faith, you often have to forgo that "Shazam!" moment and just wait a while. You might like to fix things then and there, but the Father has an unbelievably complex plan in motion for the whole of humanity. The answer to your prayer might be better delivered at a later time, and it might not always come in the form you expect.

Teach your children faith by your willingness to wait in happy assurance that God will deal with the matter. Having taken them on that journey with you, be sure to share your wonder and delight at how well and how wonderfully the Father works these matters out—in His own time and often with the minimum of showmanship.

———————◆———————

Dear God, only You know the complete picture. I know
this, and yet I still fret. Encourage me to be patient, trusting,
and reassured that You already know how all my family's needs
will be met, even if it seems a complete mystery to me. Amen.

THOSE TEENAGE YEARS

Then the man and his wife heard the sound of the Lord God
as he was walking in the garden in the cool of the day, and they
hid from the Lord God among the trees of the garden.

GENESIS 3:8 NIV

You might hear it described in some fancy church talk, but basically the Father sent Me into the world to repair a breach between Him and His children.

At first, in the "childlike" stage of humanity, God and people walked together and talked together. It was wonderful. Then, with a little help from a serpent, the children reached the teenage stage. They thought they knew better than God, and things turned sour for a long time.

It might be of some reassurance to you that the teenage years don't "just happen" in earthly families any more than they did back in the Garden of Eden. And, of course, the serpent is still at work.

So, you may think, *if God couldn't deal with those times, how am I supposed to?* But He did cope, and, as always, He set an example for you to follow. He sent Me. And I am going to step on that serpent's head.

If you need a little extra help with those teenage years, invite Me along. Of course, it might help you if I'm already a part of the family.

Gracious Jesus, thank You for my faithful wife and the
home we have raised our children in. For the times we
can't be there and for the things we can't do,
we commit them to You in trust. Amen.

ENDURING HEARTBREAK

God showed how much he loved us by sending
his one and only Son into the world so that
we might have eternal life through him.
1 JOHN 4:9 NLT

———————◆◆———————

There are few things more difficult for parents than watching their children having their hearts broken. The worst heartbreaks are those when the child loses a love he or she believed was the "real thing."

Most parents can only sit and watch as their children cry. But if you have done your job as a dad, your children already know what real love is. It will surround them, providing the security they need to get through their personal tragedy in comfort and safety.

You could look at the fall of mankind as a heartbreak. There has been a certain amount of overdramatic and self-destructive behavior since that parting. But the Father never stopped loving humankind. And to prove it, He sent me.

Do for your children what the Father does for His. Teach them that no matter how big the hurt or how great the loss, there is already, and always will be, greater loves surrounding them: yours and His.

That's how you and the Father keep the possibility of falling in love again alive.

———————◆◆———————

Amazing love and amazing grace surround me, thanks to You,
my heavenly Father. I want to share this beauty with my children,
especially in their times of hurt. May my thoughts, words,
and actions bring this desire to life. In Jesus' name I pray, amen.

GROWTH FOR A PURPOSE

*"It is like a mustard seed, which a man took and
planted in his garden. It grew and became a tree,
and the birds perched in its branches."*
LUKE 13:19 NIV

———————— ◆ ————————

Mustard seeds are tiny when they are planted, but they grow
phenomenally. Sometimes the bush can reach fifteen feet tall—
much taller than many plants in the garden that grow from much
larger seeds.

In a literal sense, it's not faith that makes the mustard seed grow so
large. But I want you to teach your little ones that faith *will* make them
grow. Through faith, and through the love of God, they will outstrip the
other "herbs" growing around them.

But be sure to point out to them that such growth must never be
for selfish ends.

The mustard bush in My parable ends up being a resting place for
many creatures and no doubt produces regular and useful crops. Teach
your children that the best and most productive way to grow is through
the kind of faith that leads to service.

And, of course, by now you know the best way to teach that truth:
outgrow the herbs in your own life.

———————— ◆ ————————

*Dear Lord, You want so much for me, so help me not to settle
for mediocrity—not for my sake, nor to my credit, but to show the
world how a godly life might be lived and to set an example that
might lead others to Your never-ending love. Amen.*

A LITTLE GIVE AND TAKE

He said, "I came naked from my mother's womb, and I will be
naked when I leave. The LORD gave me what I had, and the
Lord has taken it away. Praise the name of the LORD!"
JOB 1:21 NLT

It's a fine thing to teach your children that God will supply all their needs, and it's not a bad thing to teach them that they might have a role in positioning themselves to receive His blessings. But it's an altogether more difficult thing to show them the good in the fact that God will not only give but also take away.

You will make it easier for them by preparing them for it. Perhaps you could make a little ritual of it. When something goes away, spend some time with them giving thanks for just what a gift it was. Identify the space it left behind and encourage them to anticipate the wonderful new way in which the Father will fill that space. Show them that God doesn't take something away without an excellent reason.

It's one of those things that is easier said than done, so practice it a little yourself—even in the "small" things, like when your team's most valuable player is traded to another team.

You give and take away, Lord. But I will bless Your name every day
for all the joy in what You give and the lessons in the things
You take away, seeking always to find
Your wisdom in everything. Amen.

THE GIFT THAT REALLY KEEPS GIVING

*"Which of you fathers, if your son asks for
a fish, will give him a snake instead?"*
LUKE 11:11 NIV

Your children will ask you for a lot of things, but you can mitigate the unnecessary stuff by teaching them to look at *why* they want what they want. Are they trying to keep up with their friends? Are they trying it to impress someone?

You might save yourself some money—and raise more balanced children—by taking that route, but your bank balance will still take regular hits.

If you agree they should have the latest "whatever," you aren't going to try to fob them off with an inferior version. You want them to have the best, and you're willing to pay for it. But are you willing to pay for the very best with your time, your effort, your patience, and your perseverance?

Of all the things you give your children, nothing is nearly as wonderful (and as long-lasting) as the faith that leads to eternal life.

It won't come easily, and it won't always make you the most popular dad. But trust Me, they will one day thank you for that one gift more than any other.

---

*Revealing Lord, show me the desires of my children's hearts.
Help me to be discerning and to give more of my time than
of my money. Lead me in wisdom and truth, that I may
be a godly role model. In Your precious name, amen.*

I AM THE TRUTH

Then Jesus said to them, "The Sabbath was made to meet the needs of people, and not people to meet the requirements of the Sabbath."
MARK 2:27 NLT

———◆———

Truths are eternal. Rules, on the other hand. . .

Truths come from God, and nothing anyone can do will change them. Rules, on the other hand, are manmade and of variable quality.

As a father, you are the source of most of the rules that govern your child's life. That should make you think long and hard about them. But here's a tip: you're not God, and you should never invest your rules with Godlike authority, making them inflexible and unchangeable.

If you apply the same rules to your children when they are sixteen as you did when they were six, they might think the rules control you rather than the other way around.

Rules are tools. The wise man uses them differently in different situations.

But if they are so flexible, I hear you ask, *then how can they have any integrity?*

Because you will have made them in consultation with Me, you will have given them, for the time they are needed, the necessary ring of truth.

———◆———

*Merciful Lord, look down on me in pity when I begin to think
I know enough to set unchanging rules. Temper my stubbornness
with wisdom. Redirect my focus from me and my needs
to You and Your truths. You, not I, rule. Amen.*

A MAN OF WORTH

*"No one can serve two masters. Either you will hate the
one and love the other, or you will be devoted to the one and
despise the other. You cannot serve both God and money."*
MATTHEW 6:24 NIV

———————◆◆———————

As a father, you want your children to be successful, don't you?
But answer me this: would you rather they made a lot of money—or
that they live the kinds of lives that would leave lots of people missing
them when they are gone?

You might struggle to admit it, but you know the second option is
the best one. And you also know that the best way to encourage your
children to live that kind of life is to live it yourself.

Teach them by your example that it is better to be a person of worth
than a person of success. Rather than driving ahead to some imagined
perfect job with a satisfying income, spread yourself out. Take what you
already have and share it. Like loaves and fishes, it will go further than
you think.

Be the man who is known to many as a kind heart, as a helping
hand, as a disciple of Mine. Teach your children the true meaning of
success.

———————◆◆———————

*Gracious Father, turn my heart from worldly success. Help me
teach my children standards that will make them welcome
in Your kingdom: compassion, love, and adoration. Amen.*

POSSESSED BY POSSESSIONS

Looking at the man, Jesus felt genuine love for him. "There is still one thing you haven't done," he told him. "Go and sell all your possessions and give the money to the poor, and you will have treasure in heaven. Then come, follow me."
MARK 10:21 NLT

There's nothing wrong with owning possessions. But being owned by them is a problem. When they become a distraction or get in the way of your good work, then they become dangerous.

This is why when I sent My disciples out into the world, I told them to take only their robes and sandals.

I'm not suggesting that you send the kids off to college with just the clothes on their backs and the shoes on their feet, but you will do them a big favor if you teach them not to be slaves to their possessions. Teach them that all things come from God, all things return to God, and all things belong to God.

They, and you, are just temporary custodians tasked to do the right thing with worldly possessions. If you have to give away to a good cause something you are particularly attached to, then you will be a better man for it.

And your children will be freer because of your example.

Heavenly Father, it's a big ask, but one I know brings unimaginable blessings. Stand beside me and give me the courage to take the leap. Show me I need nothing but You in this world— so I can then show my children the same thing. Amen.

TIMES OF REBELLION

"Yet they did not listen or pay attention; they were stiff-necked and would not listen or respond to discipline."
JEREMIAH 17:23 NIV

Y ou know this already—in fact, I know you do because I watched you put your own parents through it. But there comes a time when children, in their not-quite-fully-developed wisdom, decide that they no longer need their parents and that they're going to close their ears to words of advice from "above." It's a part of growing up.

Oh, the number of times the children of Israel put the Father through that! He would save their collective skin, but before you knew it, they were all independent and worshipping other so-called gods again. Frustrating? You bet.

The Father resorted to a little discipline. He called in the Assyrians and the Babylonians. But He never abandoned the people of Israel. And, eventually, He brought them back home.

Those troubled times are often when children (or young adults) need their dad the most. So be patient and remember what it was like for you going through the same phase. And when they walk away, make sure you always leave the door open for them to come back.

Dear Lord, there is a broken streak in me. I want desperately to fix it, but I can't. So I turn it over to You. Now, when I see my child suffering in the same way, I know what the solution is. In trust, Lord, I give them to You. Amen.

SPEAK LIFE

*"But I tell you that everyone will have to give account on the
day of judgment for every empty word they have spoken."*
MATTHEW 12:36 NIV

The things you say to or in front of your children will be their window into the world. Not only will your words influence their opinions on lots of subjects, but they will also help shape the image they have of themselves.

If you tell your children negative things, the influence will last longer than the frustrations that inspired the words. Likewise with positive comments. Given that your words are so influential, it might be worth deciding on a policy for their use ahead of time. Do you want to wear your children down with them, or do you want to use them to help your children fulfill their marvelous potential?

When I invested love in people and called them beloved of the Father, they—My disciples in particular—exceeded all their own expectations.

So, given that words have power (and they undoubtedly serve either God or the other guy), ask yourself, *Will I speak death to my children— or life?*

---

*Dear Lord, I can't imagine the damage my tongue has caused my
children over the years. But I can imagine You helping me turn
that around. I would have the words of my mouth be acceptable
to You. I would have them be life-affirming and singing
praises. And I can do all that through You, Lord. Amen.*

WHO'S THAT MAN?

*"But what about you?" he asked. "Who do you say
I am?" Peter answered, "You are the Messiah."*
MARK 8:29 NIV

———— ◆ ————

People had different opinions on who I was when I walked in and around Jerusalem. Some thought I was the prophet Elijah, others thought I was John the Baptist returned from the dead. I remember asking Simon Peter who he thought I was—and being quite delighted with his answer.

Your children might ask you who you think I am, but mostly they will think they already know the answer to that question. So I need a little extra from you. Rather than have them think of Me as that guy on the cross or the guy who runs the church, I want you to tell them of the differences I have made in your life.

Sure, it might be a little embarrassing. There may be things about the man you were before we met that you don't want them to know about. Be diplomatic, but make sure they know the impact I've had.

Then when someone asks your children who they think Jesus is, they'll be able to reply, "He's a close, personal friend of my dad."

———— ◆ ————

*Sweet Lord, I blush at the memory of the times Your name
stuck in my throat. You deserve so much better from me.
I pray I have the courage, and the love, to proclaim
Your name as it deserves. You are glorious! Amen.*

CALLED INTO SERVICE

*A little farther up the shore he saw two other brothers, James
and John, sitting in a boat with their father, Zebedee, repairing
their nets. And he called them to come, too. They immediately
followed him, leaving the boat and their father behind.*
MATTHEW 4:21–22 NLT

You tell your children not to go with strangers—but would you let them go with Me?

There might come a time when your child wants to dedicate himself or herself to a life of service. It will take a lot of courage, but I imagine it will worry you more than it does your child.

You have your dreams for your children, and you know a life with Me won't offer much in the way of comfort and security. And the path they choose might not necessarily fit in with your idea of service.

Come and talk to Me about it. I'd like to have you on My side, but I appreciate how difficult it might be. Remember, though, for all your claim on them, for all the love you have invested, they are first and foremost children of the Almighty. In the long run, I can love them more and care for them better.

Trust Me with them.

*Jesus, lover of my soul, my children are my most precious possessions—
and Yours to use as You deem wise. All I ask is that You forgive
the all-too-human part of me that hesitates—
as I know You will. Amen.*

FIND ME HERE

"Then the King will say to those on his right, 'Come, you who are blessed by my Father; take your inheritance, the kingdom prepared for you since the creation of the world. For I was hungry and you gave me something to eat, I was thirsty and you gave me something to drink, I was a stranger and you invited me in.'"
MATTHEW 25:34–35 NIV

———————◆———————

How will your children recognize me? Will they think of Me as the man in the robe, as the man who floats in clouds, or the man with a halo over His head?

Or will they know to find Me among the grieving, the damaged, and the hungry?

Oh, I'll be there at home, at prayer time, on the good days and the bad. But teach them also to look for Me in any situation where love might make things better. That will take some supervision and discretion on your part, but don't let that stop you. Start with age-appropriate lessons, but encourage them to look for Me in those places. Eventually, they will go there themselves.

Your children will find Me there, and with your guidance they will recognize the real Me, not only in the people they are helping, but in their own sacrificial love.

———————◆———————

Creator of all things, let me see You in all people. Knowing that I all too often see things my way, open my eyes to Your way that I might properly lead my children to where You are. Amen.

THE GREEN-EYED MONSTER

For I am afraid that when I come I won't like what I find, and you won't like my response. I am afraid that I will find quarreling, jealousy, anger, selfishness, slander, gossip, arrogance, and disorderly behavior.
2 Corinthians 12:20 nlt

'm not saying you are a jealous guy, but as a father who might have to deal with jealousy's consequences, I am suggesting you watch out for it. Look at what happened between Sarai and Hagar, or Jacob and Esau. Some of these same kinds of battles are still being fought today.

Be jealous of nothing and accept it from no one. You have what you should have, and if someone else wants it. . .try giving it to them. They might not want it so much when they see all the attendant responsibilities. Treat everyone as equals. Love all your children the same, even though their behavior might be very different.

That's all very easy to suggest, but where would you find the security, the patience, and the confidence to do all of it?

In My love for you.

If you are secure in Me, then nothing else will be worth being jealous of or possessive over. If you are overflowing with My love, then you will have enough for everyone, with plenty left over.

If You didn't create it, Lord, then I don't need to keep it. And jealousy is surely someone else's work. May Your love and reassurance be the brooms that sweep it from my life forever. Amen.

FORGIVE ME FOR NOT FORGIVING

"And when you stand praying, if you hold anything against anyone, forgive them, so that your Father in heaven may forgive you your sins."
MARK 11:25 NIV

Have you ever noticed the scene in the opening credits of *The Simpsons* where Marge slaps the car horn—and little Maggie does the same with her junior driver set? Can I draw a lesson from that? Sure I can.

If you really lay on the horn, are you forgiving the guy who just cut in front of you? If the children are in the car, are they seeing Me in you? Do you repent of your anger later, or do you just make allowances for yourself? Would you let your children get away with the same "justifying" excuses you use?

You need to be a bigger man than that!

If Marge had exercised a little forgiveness, waved, and shouted, "Have a nice day!" in her familiar rasping voice, do you think Maggie would still have laid on that horn?

Forgiveness. There are plenty of opportunities to practice it each day. It doesn't come naturally, but your children need to see you getting better at it so they know they can, too.

Lord, You know my lack of forgiveness is simply a measure of my own insecurity. But You died for me. There is no greater security than that! Help me keep that fact in the forefront of my mind so that I may forgive graciously, as You forgive me. Amen.

SAMARITAN IN AN SUV

"Going over to him, the Samaritan soothed his wounds with olive oil and wine and bandaged them. Then he put the man on his own donkey and took him to an inn, where he took care of him."
LUKE 10:34 NLT

———————◆———————

If the priest, the Levite, and the good Samaritan in My story of the Good Samaritan had *driven* along that road that day, which one would have looked most like you?

Appeals for help by the roadside are all too common these days. Sadly, some of the people involved are out to con those whose good hearts motivate them to help out. When we see someone along the road who appears to need help, there are a lot of good reasons to keep on driving.

Of course, the priest and the Levite had good reasons as well.

Now, imagine this scenario from your little passengers' point of view. How many people do they see on those daily journeys who seem to be asking for help? And not knowing what your reasons are, how many do they see you ignoring?

What are you teaching them?

By all means, share your reasons with them. They will be a fine test of how good those reasons are. But more important than not being taken advantage of by a phony beggar is showing your children that you gladly give as you have gladly received.

———————◆———————

Sweet Jesus, make me less concerned with looking foolish and more concerned with helping those in need. After all, should I be fooled while trusting, I know You can use that to change a heart. May all my efforts be in Your name. Amen.

PAYING CAESAR

And he asked them, "Whose image is this? And whose inscription?"
"Caesar's," they replied. Then he said to them, "So give back to
Caesar what is Caesar's, and to God what is God's."
MATTHEW 22:20–21 NIV

───────◆───────

I don't imagine your children are interested in your taxes. But I'm sure they would be happier not having their parents pursued by the IRS.

How you deal with your tax return often reflects how you deal with life in general. You pay for a ton of stuff, but what do you take for free that you shouldn't? And what seemingly trivial things do your children see you getting away with?

Teaching them to cheat the system, in whatever way, might seem like a good idea at times, but it's still teaching them to cheat. And they don't have to. You don't have to.

Different societies have different requirements of their citizens. Just as I expect you to serve and be honest wherever you are, so I expect you to pay your way. And teach the next generation to do so as well.

What? You can't afford it? Ask Me. If you need it, I will supply it. If you don't. . .well, better to do without it than have Me, and them, see you lower your standards.

───────◆───────

Build up my faith that I may better trust You in all things,
setting an example for my children in all my dealings.
Please help me to be a righteous man, Lord. Amen.

ASPIRE TO BE BETTER

*"Now repent of your sins and turn to God,
so that your sins may be wiped away."*
ACTS 3:19 NLT

———————— ◆ ————————

Dear child, I know you don't always practice what you preach. I know about the lapses you manage to hide from everyone else. I also know you set a fine example in many ways, and that's important to Me. But how much of the good work you have done would turn permanently to dust if your family realized that you don't have the same expectations of yourself that you do of them?

Know this: no one is perfect. Everyone slacks off from time to time. You, at least, are ahead of the game in aspiring to be better.

The danger is that when you know there is little chance of you being found out, those "slips" become permanent. Perhaps it would help knowing that I see them, and that every time I see them I wish better for you next time.

Want better for yourself. Accept your weaknesses—but don't settle for them. You are journeying heavenward, and that means you don't get to sit still. And every little bad habit you discard along the way brings you closer to home.

———————— ◆ ————————

*The enemy is dangerously unobtrusive, Lord. He ties me down
in such small ways that I don't even notice. But I will not be his
servant, and I will not give him my family. Through Your power,
Lord, and in Your glorious name, we will be free. Amen.*

GOD SWINGS MY BAT

I praise you because I am fearfully and wonderfully made;
your works are wonderful, I know that full well.
PSALM 139:14 NIV

———————◆———————

I t's fun to take the credit. It's quite an ego boost to have your children think you are capable of all things and the fount of all knowledge. But you know it's not serious. Right?

The thing is, the little ones are only too ready to believe it of their daddy. But that leads them to wonder why they aren't all those things when their turn comes.

Give them a break by easing the pressure on yourself—and teach them a lesson at the same time.

If you swing a good bat, tell your children it's a God-given ability and that He gave you good health as well. If you know some amazing stuff, tell them God did a wonderful job designing the brain. If you can give them a comfortable lifestyle, let them know who gave it to you. And each time you tell them something, don't forget to give thanks.

Oh, and one more thing. Teach your children that even though God supplies all things and is deserving of all thanks, as His creations, you are still wonderfully made. And so are they!

———————◆———————

What could I do without You, Lord? Breathe? I don't think so.
So let me with the very breath You gave me proclaim that
You are my all in all, my beginning, my end,
and everything in between. Amen.

DON'T GET EVEN, GET BETTER

"But I warn you—unless your righteousness is better than the righteousness of the teachers of religious law and the Pharisees, you will never enter the Kingdom of Heaven!"
MATTHEW 5:20 NLT

The opportunities to make less of yourself are almost limitless—but each one of them is also a chance to better yourself.

It's all in how you look at the words. Like a bully on a playground, the devil provokes us in every aspect of our lives.

I know it's heartbreaking for you to see your kids hurting—and to know who seems to be responsible. But what good do you do charging around and rewarding pain with more pain? When you do that, you teach children that the best response to evil is to do evil in return—which is why evil continues.

Raise your children to be overcomers. Teach them why bad things sometimes happen and how best to overcome them. Of course, that best way is moving closer to Me. With My help, you can only rise up. The bullies—and their boss—will only wail and gnash their teeth in frustration as we rise.

And all because you took My advice and decided not to play their game.

Lord, I am a flawed man with a strong desire to be a godly man. You, Jesus, are the bridge I need to cross. Step in front of me, Lord, the next time I react to evil in my old habitual way. Amen.

GOD'S GIFT TO YOU

*A wife of noble character who can find? She is
worth far more than rubies. Her husband has full
confidence in her and lacks nothing of value.*
PROVERBS 31:10–11 NIV

———————◆———————

Imagine a powerful man gave you a wonderful gift. Would you trash it
in front of him?

Your wife might not have come to you wrapped in a ribbon, and you
weren't given to her in a box full of Styrofoam. But you are each other's
gift from God. If she doesn't seem to you like a gift from God, then you
need to look at how you treat her and determine if you show her the
appreciation fitting such a gift.

Children's mothers occupy a unique place in their hearts. As much
as they love Dad, there's no one like Mom. How you treat that
representative of God's love matters hugely to them. And to Him.

No marriage is perfect, but each one has the potential to be as close
to perfect as this world allows. So when problems crop up (and they
will), turn to God for help. Together.

And don't forget to add that magic ingredient every gift should
receive: a healthy dollop of appreciation. It works wonders, and it sets
a great example.

———————◆———————

*Lord, deep down, I know I don't deserve the wonderful gift You've given
me in my wife. But I don't deserve You either, yet You still love me.
Help me to be the husband my wife deserves and a father
who loves his children extravagantly. Amen.*

THOSE CASUAL CONDEMNATIONS

"Do not judge others, and you will not be judged. For you will be treated as you treat others. The standard you use in judging is the standard by which you will be judged."
MATTHEW 7:1–2 NLT

———— ◆ ————

Think for a moment about the last time someone did something you would never have expected of them—something that disappointed you deeply.

Those times should teach you something about the folly of judging others. No one knows the heart of a person—no one but the Father and Me, that is. That's why you should never see your opinions about another's behavior as fact. It's also why you should always be prepared to change your mind.

After all, if many people really were what others thought they were, then there would be no point in Me being here—no point in redemption.

Prejudging people is easy. Some people do it several times a day through the thoughtless comments they make about other people in front of their children. And the children accept those parental opinions as. . .well. . .gospel.

Those might seem like throwaway comments to you, and difficult to prevent, but that doesn't make them any less damaging.

The old saying goes, "If you can't say something good, say nothing at all," but I prefer, "If you can't say anything good. . .look deeper and try harder!"

———— ◆ ————

Lord, help me to encourage my children to take a greater interest in people and to get to know their hearts. Once they know their hearts, I am sure they will see You in every one of them. Amen.

WEED OR WAIT

"The farmer's workers went to him and said, 'Sir, the field where you planted that good seed is full of weeds! Where did they come from?' 'An enemy has done this!' the farmer exclaimed. 'Should we pull out the weeds?' they asked. 'No,' he replied, 'you'll uproot the wheat if you do.'"
MATTHEW 13:27–29 NLT

———◆◆———

I n the garden of every life some weeds will grow. Some will be unsightly and, depending on how highly you prize that garden, upsetting. And they can sometimes be difficult to get at without trampling on some flowers.

Okay. Enough of the garden analogy.

Despite your best efforts, it is almost inevitable that some bad habits or unpleasant traits will take root, perhaps temporarily, in your children's lives. They simply won't be able to avoid them all, no matter how well you prepare them.

The question then becomes, *How will you respond to those weeds?*

God willing, there will be many weeds you can tackle without harming the relationship. But, like the farmer in My parable, you might need to wait a while and put up with a few "tares" for the sake of the good crop that will come.

Patience and perseverance are a gardener's greatest assets. And an ugly habit's surest cure.

———◆◆———

Lord, help me identify the devil's work. And, having recognized it, let me always turn to You for help in dealing with it. Keep me from blindly rushing into his trap. Show me the better, greater way. Amen.

THE UNDESERVED GIFT

Because of his grace he declared us righteous and
gave us confidence that we will inherit eternal life.
TITUS 3:7 NLT

———————◆◆◆———————

Do you want to see some real surprise on your children's faces? Wait until they have misbehaved one time too many and your patience has reached its limit. Wait until they know what's coming— and until they know they deserve it. Then hug them, tell them you love them, and get on with what you were doing.

Does that sound like I'm saying you should be a soft touch? Well, I'm not suggesting you do it all the time, but I am suggesting that you be the one to first acquaint them with grace. You know. . .undeserved love.

It goes against all reason and intuition, but you may find that it works wonders in them.

You won't need to use it often, but your children need to know it exists.

You should have seen Saul's (later the apostle Paul) face when I stood before him in my glory and power. He fully expected to be blasted. The last thing he expected was to be loved, but that's exactly what I did for him. And he went on to do wonderful work for My Father's kingdom.

Just don't scare your children as much as I did him!

———————◆◆◆———————

Lord, I could spend the rest of my life seeking to understand grace.
But instead I choose to be amazed by it and humbly accept it. My thanks
are hardly adequate, Lord, for the gift of Your grace. But on behalf of
me, my family, and all your children. . .thank You anyway. Amen.

CARRY LOVE, NOT THE OTHER STUFF

"Take my yoke upon you and learn from me, for I am gentle and humble in heart, and you will find rest for your souls. For my yoke is easy and my burden is light."
MATTHEW 11:29–30 NIV

Imagine a picture of an old-fashioned milkmaid. She'll have a pretty frilled cap on her head and a wooden yoke across her shoulders. The buckets of milk on either end of the yoke look heavy, but she will be smiling because carrying them on the yoke is a lot easier than carrying them by hand.

The work has to be done. The milk has to be brought from the barn to the market. She could have chosen the more difficult way to do it, but she didn't.

As head of the house (with Mom's expert advice), you set your children's chores. You shouldn't stand by watching them doing their chores the hard way, unless it's to teach them that there is an easier way.

You know better than your children that there are two kinds of work being done in this world—the Father's and the enemy's. . .love and its opposite. The milk gets to the market, or it goes sour.

When your children work (and they must), be the man who shows them that the devil's yoke only *looks* lighter.

Lord, Your yoke is easy, but the path I walk is full of distractions and diversions. Remind me whose work it is so that I might reach for that yoke and wear it happily forever. Amen.

THE LAST LESSON

Jesus said, "Father, forgive them, for they do not know what they are doing." And they divided up his clothes by casting lots.
LUKE 23:34 NIV

───◆───

I f they knew what he's done, they would understand why I don't talk to him."

"Well, I tried. I'm not going to go chasing him. He can just rot."

"He'll only do it again. That's what he's like. So, I'm never giving him the chance."

You know that one guy—the one you are never going to reach out to? Your children probably don't even know what he did. They also don't know that he's your exception to the rule of forgiveness.

But they know how to make excuses like the ones above. *Everyone* knows those excuses. And at some point in their lives, they will probably use the very same ones.

So imagine if you told them about that guy—told them how much you hated him but how you overcame that hate, put those excuses aside, and forgave him. Imagine if you could—after all that—introduce him to your children as a friend.

How powerful an example would that be? And it would teach them what I tried to teach from the cross—that there are no exceptions to the rule of forgiveness.

───◆───

I have no excuse, gracious Lord. I know the joy of Your forgiveness, but still I resist forgiving others. Walk with me at those moments, Lord. Point to my own unforgiven ones— and remind me how much You love them. Amen.

THE ANTIDOTE TO FEAR

There is no fear in love. But perfect love drives
out fear, because fear has to do with punishment.
The one who fears is not made perfect in love.
1 JOHN 4:18 NIV

———— ◆ ————

D o you like the idea of letting your children see you really afraid?
I think not.

Have you ever *been* really afraid? I'm sorry for even reminding you of it.

Fear is a big deal for people, which is why the Father and I peppered the Bible with the words "Do not fear!"

First, fear is the work of the enemy. He creates it then uses it against you. Second, there is no need for fear, because your life is in My hands. Some awkward, embarrassing, painful things might happen to you, but they will be preludes to better things. The devil uses fear to take away that certainty, offering nothing good in return.

All this reassurance doesn't mean you won't feel fear; it's meant to encourage you to draw closer to Me when you do. Once you learn I am always there for you and am a constant source of strength and comfort, even in the most difficult situations, then you can bring your children to that place.

Talk to them about fear. Then show them the cure for it.

———— ◆ ————

If everything were taken from me, sweet Jesus, I would
still have You. I know that—but I haven't mastered it yet.
Strengthen my resolve, Lord. Help me teach my children
that the opposite of fear is trust in You. Amen.

TALK BIBLE LIKE A NATIVE

*They said to each other, "Didn't our hearts
burn within us as he talked with us on the road
and explained the Scriptures to us?"*
LUKE 24:32 NLT

———◆———

When modern-day "explorers" go into areas they aren't familiar with, they often hire a native guide who knows his way around. In reality, the area being explored is often new only to the explorer.

Your children may view the Bible with a certain amount of trepidation. They know its reputation; they have seen influential people hold it in high regard. But it can seem to them a little like unexplored territory—with highlands and lowlands, dense in some areas, easier in others, beautiful in some places, and scary in others.

What they need is someone to walk through it with them—their very own native guide.

How do those guides become so invaluable to the modern-day explorers? They live there, walk the territory often, and know it like the back of their hand.

You can be that same kind of guide for your children when they ask. So spend as much time as you can there. That way, you can be thought of as a native in God's country.

———◆———

*Lord, if I am to be a guide in Your Word, I only dare because
You are a guide to me. Be the lamp of illumination by which
I read scripture to my children. As I teach them, I pray that
the Author of it all will always be teaching me. Amen.*

IN TOUCH WITH THE WILD

After sending them home, he went up into the hills by himself to pray. Night fell while he was there alone.
MATTHEW 14:23 NLT

———◆———

O kay, you're a civilized guy. You work hard and are educated, well-spoken, responsible, respectably dressed, a careful driver, and an attentive husband.

But there's more.

You were made to be a good man in a variety of situations. You fit well(ish) in the modern world, but part of you is also designed for more basic situations: like taking care of people and providing in a wilder environment.

That side of you also needs some attention. If "wild man" is content, "modern man" will be better.

There were times I took Myself away from the crowd and their expectations, so I understand that need. So do yourself a favor: among all your daddy duties, factor in some time for you to simply be. Take to the hills, or the lake, or the woods. Get back in touch with yourself, renew your appreciation of creation, and spend time in conversation with God.

Then, when you feel ready, be the good dad you just can't help being and share that experience with your children.

———◆———

Father, man was born of dust and outside of the garden, so it's not surprising he sometimes needs to be "out there." Loving Creator, I thank You that You have made so many places where I can reconnect with You so I can then help my children reconnect with Your creation. May we find You everywhere. Amen.

A MAN OF SOME ACCOUNT

"If your brother or sister sins, go and point out their fault, just between the two of you. If they listen to you, you have won them over."
MATTHEW 18:15 NIV

———————◆———————

Y ou are a man under authority, ultimately answerable to the Father. But admit it—in the short term, you can be prone to ignoring My corrections.

No one likes being told he is wrong. Your children don't like it, but you do it for them because it's important that they learn from their mistakes, important that they grow and get ever better.

But when you are the boss, the head of the family, who gets to tell you when you are wrong? Unpleasant as it may be, you need to know about those times. So find yourself an accountability partner. Make it someone you respect, someone who won't put up with any of your nonsense. And you perform the same function for him.

Find a way to meet regularly and spend time in honest conversation. Forget about the weather, ignore the football, and talk about matters that matter.

If all goes well, you will end up listening to Me more, but until then find another friend to keep you accountable.

———————◆———————

Dear Lord, You know my shortcomings, and I know I would
be a better husband and father if I acknowledged them.
Send me that man who will tell me the truth. And please,
Lord, sit on my pride while I listen to him. Amen.

DEATH AS A BEGINNING

Then, when our dying bodies have been transformed into bodies that will never die, this Scripture will be fulfilled: "Death is swallowed up in victory. O death, where is your victory? O death, where is your sting?"
1 CORINTHIANS 15:54–55 NLT

——————◆——————

S ometimes fathers have to deal with some heavy subjects. Like death.

Pets die, neighbors die, distant relatives die. It makes an impact, but—thankfully—only an occasional one. But it can be traumatic for your children when death comes closer to home.

You can ease that sense of shock by raising your children to know that death is only a prelude to life. For example, teach them that the apple falls from the tree and rots so that the seed can become a tree. Assure them that spring always follows winter. And so on, at every opportunity.

But most of all, tell them that I am the life in death. Assure them about heaven. Tell them it's okay to miss people and to be sad when they pass away. But also tell them about races well run, victory in the end, and the real happy ever after.

Take the sting out of death for your children by telling them that, through Me, there is ultimately no such thing.

——————◆——————

It's a scary thing, Lord, and something we don't get to practice. But we have Your assurance that physical death is but a passing event, soon to be forgotten in the everlasting glory of eternal life with You. Forgive us our hesitation, and welcome us home. Amen.

BEYOND DISNEYLAND

I have fought the good fight, I have finished the race, I have kept the faith. Now there is in store for me the crown of righteousness, which the Lord, the righteous Judge, will award to me on that day— and not only to me, but also to all who have longed for his appearing.
2 TIMOTHY 4:7–8 NIV

———— ◆ ————

Imagine telling your family that you were taking them for an eight-hundred-mile drive—to a parking lot somewhere. Imagine the lack of enthusiasm! They would probably begin the trip already bored, and their behavior would only get worse as the hours passed.

Something similar happens with many who have no hope of heaven. Faced with lives with no point or purpose, some turn to alcohol, drugs, lawlessness, and other vices. With no real purpose in life, why would they do anything else?

But a sense of purpose throws a different light on the decisions that shape a life. Just as children on a long drive to Disneyland or to the beach would probably be a delight to travel with, people who have real purpose in life are more likely to be pleasant to be around.

I know you would never tell your children that there is no point to life (or no God), but don't just leave it at that. Always remind them that I have given them a wonderful purpose and an awesome destination for their trip through life. It will make the journey better for everyone.

———— ◆ ————

The life and the world You gave us, Lord, is far too complex to be pointless. Give me the wit to understand this and explain it to my children. Amen.

STRONGER TOGETHER

*They devoted themselves to the apostles' teaching and to fellowship,
to the breaking of bread and to prayer. Everyone was filled with awe
at the many wonders and signs performed by the apostles.*
ACTS 2:42 NIV

———————◆———————

Guys tend to think they can do things by themselves. The question, "Would you like a hand with that?" often inspires the very male response, "Are you saying I can't handle it myself?"

Hey, I know you're tough. The Father knew I was tough when He sent Me on my mission. First thing I did? Gather a bunch of friends to help Me. You're not going to mock Me for that, are you? Well, cut yourself the same kind of slack.

You can do a lot of stuff on your own, but a bunch of individuals won't achieve as much for the kingdom as a community will. There's just more love in a community of true believers, and that makes it much greater than the sum of its parts. In a way, it's a glimpse of what is to come in heaven.

So add your special abilities to your church groups or fellowship gatherings. You will benefit, and the group will benefit. Those you work with will be a blessing to your children, and you will be a blessing to theirs.

———————◆———————

*Father God, make me a blessing to many, and help me lay
aside the pride that prevents me from letting them be a
blessing to me in return. And help me show my children
that we really are part of Your larger family. Amen.*

REACH OUT TO A STRANGER

Do not forget to show hospitality to strangers, for by so doing some people have shown hospitality to angels without knowing it.
HEBREWS 13:2 NIV

◆

For your children's own safety, I want you to teach them "stranger danger," but I don't want you to practice it yourself.

One of the saddest things I see in humankind is the fact that so many brothers and sisters are strangers to each other. Sure, there are times when the stranger should be feared, but the enemy blows that fear out of proportion so that strangers who might once have been invited home for dinner no longer are.

The little ones need to be kept safe, but at the same time it will do them good to see you reaching out, offering a helping hand, or speaking to someone you have never met like an old friend. Because, always remember, those strangers are no less dear to Me than your children are to you.

Set the example, so that when your little charges become fully grown adults, they won't hesitate to see the world as the kind of place where there is no such thing as a stranger—only family members they haven't yet met.

◆

Lord, fear has taught us to wear masks and to not look beyond them. I ask that Your love equips us to go into the world unmasked and to see through the masks others wear, enabling us to better love one another. In Jesus' name, amen.

THANK YOU FOR THANKFULNESS

I will give thanks to the LORD because of his righteousness;
I will sing the praises of the name of the LORD Most High.
PSALM 7:17 NIV

———————◆◆———————

G iving thanks—when done properly—can be one more thing to be
thankful for.

If you offer up thanks to God halfheartedly, or as part of some
routine, it can become more like a chore, something almost to be
resented.

But a heartfelt "thank You" is a reminder to yourself, as well as the
Father, that you have been given something worthwhile. And that,
in turn, reminds you that *you* are worthwhile.

The more you give thanks, the more you find to be thankful for.
And the more you find to be thankful for, the more you are aware of the
Father's great love for you.

Ask yourself which kind of life you would prefer for your children—
one of selfish expectation, or one of thankful appreciation. If you want
your children to understand the blessings of being thankful, you have
to show it to them in how you live. And you could always start by giving
thanks for the opportunity to be their father.

———————◆◆———————

Be patient with me, God, for there is so much I haven't thanked You for.
But I will do my best while I'm alive on this earth. After that,
heavenly Father, I will be thanking You forever. Amen.

LOVE LONGS TO GIVE

And we are confident that he hears us whenever
we ask for anything that pleases him.
1 JOHN 5:14 NLT

———————————◆———————————

Tell me, why would you refuse to give your child something?

Here are some valid reasons: You can't afford it. It might be damaging to them in some way. There is some lesson your children can learn from being denied it.

Does that about cover it?

Laying aside all those factors, you would give your children anything, wouldn't you? Because you love them and love longs to give.

Now, your children may not understand your longing to give on an intellectual level, but they know it on a heart level.

How about you? Do you feel the same way about your heavenly Father's ability and willingness to give as your children do about yours?

The worst move children can make when they are denied something is to throw a tantrum. Of course, you would never do that if, say, you didn't get the job you were pinning your hopes on. Would you?

You're a father of children and a child of the Father, so I want you to understand (and teach) that God may have very good reasons for not giving you what you want. Because, as I mentioned, love longs to give.

———————————◆———————————

Father, I understand Your reasons for giving as poorly as my children
comprehend mine. I don't ask for more possessions, or even for more
understanding. I ask for more trust. And one more thing: let my
children see me trusting my Father. In Jesus' name, amen.

INVESTING IN FREEDOM

Anyone who does not provide for their relatives, and especially for their own household, has denied the faith and is worse than an unbeliever.
1 TIMOTHY 5:8 NIV

———— ◆ ————

"Why should I worry about being careful with my cash?" you might ask. "Wouldn't a God who loves me just give me more when I run out?"

Do you remember the Bible passage that tells us that just because God forgives all sins, we aren't to go on racking up sin? (If not, look up Romans 6:1–2.) Same principle.

The Bible calls on you to be a good steward with the things God gives you. Why? Well, there's the things good stewardship does *for* you, and the things the other kind does *to* you.

Good stewardship promotes thought, responsibility, and forward planning. (And until the kingdom comes, we should be all about forward planning.) Bad stewardship, on the other hand, promotes living for the moment and leaves you open to debt, temptation, and lots of other traps.

Which would you choose for your children?

The best thing a good steward can do is produce more good stewards. Start teaching your children fiscal responsibility when they are young. Financial freedom enables you, and them, to give and live freely.

That's surely a long-term investment worth making for your children.

———— ◆ ————

Father, the love of money is the root of all evil, so give me wisdom in my dealing with it. Help me avoid its many traps and temptations. Teach me to see money as yet another tool to be used for Your glory. Amen.

GOD IN YOUR GIVING

*"But when you give to someone in need, don't let your
left hand know what your right hand is doing."*
MATTHEW 6:3 NLT

━━━━━━━━━━ ◆ ━━━━━━━━━━

The Bible seems quite down on doing good deeds so they can be seen publically, doesn't it? And yet as a dad you are expected to set a good example in such things. What's with that?

Well, it's not that We want good things kept secret. It's just that We don't want them done for the wrong reasons. Some people just like to show the world how "good" they are, and others are addicted to the "buzz" of helping. Neither group has God at the heart of what they are doing.

By all means, let your children see you in your charitable works, but show them that it is nothing more than you would normally do, that it's really no big deal—except that it's God's work. Show them that you aren't giving anything He didn't give to you and that you aren't caring any more than a fraction of the amount you have been cared for.

Teach your children not to be good deed junkies. Instead show them that God wants them to be agents of His justice, distributors of His property, and administrators of His love.

━━━━━━━━━━ ◆ ━━━━━━━━━━

*Father, I have nothing to give that You didn't give me. Let me be Your
hands in this world, and always remind me that the credit is all Yours.
When I help, make my face invisible. Shine through me
so my children and others see only You. Amen.*

THE FALL AND RISE

He told them, "This is what is written: The Messiah will
suffer and rise from the dead on the third day."
LUKE 24:46 NIV

———————————◆———————————

As children grow, their falls become less about tripping over their
own feet and more about moral or behavioral stumbles. The falls
become less about inability to stay on their feet and more about letting
themselves down.

That doesn't always stop at childhood.

Each time children let themselves down, they are as disappointed in
themselves as anyone. That disappointment can erode their self-belief.
If that keeps up, eventually they will fall down and stay down because
they don't believe they can do any better.

You can help with this. Your children see you as a rock of certainty.
If you can teach them by telling them you went through a similar
experience and still got back up, it will help show them the way. Of
course, you won't always be able to help, and in those kinds of situations
the best you can do is point them to the One who gave you that helping
hand in your darkest hour, after your heaviest fall.

Remind your children that they serve the King of rising again. And
what I did through the power of the Father—rise from the dead—I will
certainly do for them.

———————————◆———————————

God above, You see me fall and don't pick me up. You leave me to
depend on Jesus, but sometimes I lean on my own strength—and I fall
again. Help me teach my children to avoid that pitfall. Amen.

A SORRY RULER

Then Saul admitted to Samuel, "Yes, I have sinned. I have disobeyed your instructions and the LORD's command, for I was afraid of the people and did what they demanded."
1 SAMUEL 15:24 NLT

Being an authority figure who never makes mistakes is more than difficult—it's impossible.

So do you want your children to see you as someone who is always right (as attractive as that may seem to your ego), or as someone who acknowledges right and wrong?

With the best intentions in the world, there have been times when you have said the wrong things to your children or come to the wrong conclusion. So what should you do?

It's tempting to say, "Go with it. Say nothing. What's to be gained by telling them Daddy made a mistake?"

Well, here's what's to be gained. Your children will see a good example of a humble man. They will know their father values truth and justice. And should you bring yourself to ask their forgiveness, they will learn from you how to ask it from the Father.

It's all of that against your pride. . .and you know what I think of pride.

So don't be wrong by always insisting you are right, be right by admitting that (once in a while) you are wrong.

Humble me, Lord. If I can't admit a mistake to my children, then I think too much of myself. It's not my authority I need to impress them with but Yours. Amen.

LOVE THE QUEEN

Jesus knew their thoughts and said to them: "Any kingdom divided against itself will be ruined, and a house divided against itself will fall."
LUKE 11:17 NIV

———— ◆ ◆ ————

Imagine a castle in merry olde England. There's a village within its outer walls and the villagers live peaceful and prosperous lives. And did I mention the king and queen are happily married?

Now imagine the same place, but the king and queen hate each other. Both would have their supporters who would hate one other. People would be busy plotting for influence, playing one ruler against the other. There would be occasional battles between the two sides. Casualties would occur and charity would fly far from the place.

Which set of villagers do you think would count themselves the most blessed?

You might not have thrones in your home, or swords, but a very similar scenario could play out in your family. You and your sweetheart won't agree on everything, but it's in your villagers' (oops. . .children's) interest that you present a united front.

That doesn't mean you always get your way by royal decree. It involves discussion, respect, a little compromise—and contented, reassured children.

If you want to be king in your home, best keep in with the queen.

———— ◆ ◆ ————

Heavenly Father, You gave me my wife and me to each other for good reasons. May I never stop searching for and discovering those reasons. May she always be a blessing in my life, and may I always be a blessing in hers. Amen.

AGAINST ALL LOGIC

"So he got up and went to his father. But while he was still a long
way off, his father saw him and was filled with compassion for him;
he ran to his son, threw his arms around him and kissed him."
LUKE 15:20 NIV

I magine you had a secret to confess to your wife. You are horrified
by the pain your admission will cause her. You hesitate, prevaricate,
perhaps lie a little, and draw it out. Why? Because against all logic,
you hope she will somehow know what is in your heart, wrap you in
her arms, and tell you it's okay.

You may not have anything like that to confess, but imagine being a
child whose mistake has taken on nightmarish proportions.

If your child takes a step toward an admission of a mistake,
don't wait so that you can teach him or her a lesson. When you see the
struggle, go to the child. You don't need to say it's okay, but you should
say that it will be. Your child's response to your generosity will be so
much more than the response to your sternness.

Does that seem a bit soft?

It might—but only until you stand before the ultimate authority
figure. He is really scary—until He catches a glimpse of a repentant
heart. Then, against all logic, He will run to you.

Father in heaven, thank You for running to me when, in my
shame, I could barely bring myself to walk. I pray that I can
do the same for others—especially my children. Amen.

THE FLOWER OF APPRECIATION

"They confronted me in the day of my disaster, but the
LORD was my support. He brought me out into a spacious
place; he rescued me because he delighted in me."
2 SAMUEL 22:19–20 NIV

When they are first born, children are little bundles of potential. Do you remember how long you stood there just gazing at your newborn son or daughter, thinking about what that little one would become?

Good nutrition helps them grow physically and sound teaching helps them grow spiritually, but do you know what causes them to really blossom, to flower into all they were meant to be? Appreciation—love expressed as delight.

If you aren't showing your children appreciation, then what are you putting in all that work for? You might need to look again at your definition of fatherhood. (You'd better believe the Father above is appreciating you.)

But temper that appreciation with wisdom and a little necessary discipline. It will pay off in the long term as your children grow into the wonderful people God intended them to be—leaving you even more to appreciate.

Parenting isn't always hard work. Make sure you mix a healthy amount of delight in with your other responsibilities.

Father, I get jaded and see Your works dimly at times. Open my eyes
to the glory of every aspect of Your creation—most particularly in
my own family, And help me help my children to see themselves
as You do, through eyes of love and appreciation. Amen.

THE WORD FOREVER

"Heaven and earth will disappear,
but my words will never disappear."
MATTHEW 24:35 NLT

E ternity rings. Engagement rings. Wedding rings. Gold is supposed to be incorruptible, and diamonds are among the strongest materials known to man. The circular shape of the rings themselves are supposed to indicate "forever"—if you run a finger around their edges, you never reach an end.

But how many of those beautiful baubles have fallen down the waste disposal? How many are left behind on vacation? How many simply disappear? The loss of the ring doesn't affect your love for your wife. You are still in it "till death us do part."

What about your children, though? You will always love them, but you aren't going to give them the same jewelry you gave your wife.

Well, I can suggest something a little less sparkly but a lot longer lasting. Teach them the words of their Savior. Memorize with them. Recite, repeat, and explore them together. They are only words, but in the beginning was the Word and at the end will be the Word.

As tokens of love intended to last an eternity, I don't think you can beat that.

Lord, help me not be distracted by superficial things. A ring is
just a ring, but the words in red are the secret of life. Remind me,
Lord, the next time I want to give my family gifts, that heavenly crowns
are the only adornments that really last for eternity. Amen.

GIVEN BACK TO THE GIVER

And when Jesus had cried with a loud voice, he said, Father, into thy
hands I commend my spirit: and having said thus, he gave up the ghost.
LUKE 23:46 KJV

"Father, into thy hands I commend my spirit."

Do you think my Father needed Me to say that? I was there on His business. He knew My heart like no man ever knew another. My spirit was already His.

But almost two thousand years ago, someone heard Me say that, and the example those words set still has power today.

What was the last thing you commended to God? And did your children hear you do it?

It's not necessary for you to wait until your last breath. Let your children hear you commend a road trip to His care. When one of them leaves the house, commend his or her safety to God. As you lay them down to sleep, as you set out for a day's work, as you prepare for an important purchase. . .and so on.

Every aspect of your life is worth giving to God in trust. Offer Him your most menial task and see what He makes of it.

As your children see what He makes of those requests, it will become more and more likely that they, in their turn, will devote their lives to Him.

Heavenly Father, the more I commit to You, the more I am Your man.
Lord, in every detail, large and small, let me declare myself Yours. Amen.

A MAN OF INFLUENCE

As he considered this, an angel of the Lord appeared
to him in a dream. "Joseph, son of David," the angel said,
"do not be afraid to take Mary as your wife. For the
child within her was conceived by the Holy Spirit."
MATTHEW 1:20 NLT

***

Most dads would like their children to think they are men of influence—movers and shakers.

Let Me tell you about my earthly father, Joseph. The little the world knows about him was because of what he did by his own volition. The Bible unfailingly recalls that he did the will of God, again and again, even in circumstances of threat and disgrace.

And now he is known throughout all the nations as the man who helped bring eternal life to the world. Joseph wasn't an extraordinary man, but God the Father already knew of his faith before He chose him to care for Me. We think of him as a mover and shaker.

You might go out and be a big noise in the world. Your children might be hugely impressed with your power and influence. But the most important thing you can do for them will be bringing them to Me—to their own eternal life.

How much more influence would you like to have?

***

Dear Lord, let me always seek to have no influence but
Your influence, no power but Your power, and no love
but Your love. In Jesus' name, amen.

FRUIT FOR THE FAMILY

But the fruit of the Spirit is love, joy, peace, forbearance,
kindness, goodness, faithfulness, gentleness and self-control.
Against such things there is no law.
GALATIANS 5:22–23 NIV

When you were going through that growth spurt in your teenage years, did you keep track of your height, impressed as you did something you had no control over—namely, growing physically?

Well, there are other kinds of growth than the purely physical, and you do have some control over these areas. These are areas of your children's lives in which you can teach them to develop.

I'm thinking of the fruit of the Spirit. As you and your children walk longer with Me, there should be noticeable improvements in your love, joy, peace, forbearance, kindness, goodness, faithfulness, gentleness, and self-control.

But keeping track of that progress is difficult to do by yourself. You might think you are the most forbearing person in the world—it's just that other folks are really annoying. Which is why you and your children need to work together with Me on this one.

It will be fun deciding how to carry out the measurements. One thing's for sure: it won't be as simple as pencil marks on the door frame.

Lord, I am not the man of God I want to be, and there is so much
about You I would have my children know. It's a challenge I want
to rise to. Thank You for providing so many wonderful ways
for us to develop our spiritual muscles. Amen.

LIVE IN LOVE

*"For this is how God loved the world: He gave his one
and only Son, so that everyone who believes in him
will not perish but have eternal life."*
JOHN 3:16 NLT

———————◆———————

You wouldn't want your children to doubt your love for them,
would you?

I've heard you say you never doubt My love for you. So, what's with
all the doubts, fears, and feelings of not being good enough?

You know whose work that is, don't you?

The Father's creations are far too amazing to merit that kind of
doubt. So how can I show you how much God loves you?

I suppose I could die for you. Oh, wait. . .I did! But not so you should
doubt you are worth it. You would make the same sacrifice for your
children, and you wouldn't want them to feel bad about it. You would
want them to see it as a measure of how deeply you love them.

Likewise!

I gave My all for you, not so you could live in the shadow of the
enemy's work but so you could live forever and be loved forever.

So try seeing yourself as your children see you. . .and as the Father
sees you. Raise your head and walk forever in My love.

———————◆———————

*Beautiful Savior, I simply can't repay You for Your sacrifice for me.
But if it is acceptable to You, I will try to live always in Your love
and spend my life bringing others closer to You. Amen.*

PREPARED TO SOAR

On the day of Pentecost all the believers were meeting
together in one place. Suddenly, there was a sound from heaven
like the roaring of a mighty windstorm, and it filled the house
where they were sitting. Then, what looked like flames or
tongues of fire appeared and settled on each of them.
ACTS 2:1–3 NLT

———————◆———————

There eventually comes a time when you either send your children into the world or they leave on their own. No matter how much you might be looking forward to the peace, seeing your children leave is still an emotional experience.

But baby eagles were made to soar and swoop, not to stay forever in the nest.

As their father, you will always be there for them. But as time goes on, they will come to rely more and more on themselves. Or so it seems. Actually, they are relying more and more on the things you taught them and the resources you provided them.

So it is up to you to ensure that those lessons and resources are of the best quality—meaning they are of God.

I knew My disciples weren't ready to go on without Me as they prepared to go out into a hostile world. That's why I told them to wait for the Holy Spirit to come and equip them.

Do likewise for your little disciples.

———————◆———————

Father, in Jesus' name I ask You to dress my children in your heavenly
protection. Arm them with Your truth. Guide and guard them through
this hostile world. Then see them safely home again. Amen.

AN IDOL KIND OF LOVE

*"So do not corrupt yourselves by making an
idol in any form—whether of a man or a woman,
an animal on the ground, a bird in the sky."*
DEUTERONOMY 4:16–17 NLT

———————◆◆———————

Can you love your children too much? No. Can you love them the wrong way? That's a different question with a different answer.

I know you have seen children whose behavior inspires sighs and rolled eyes from everyone but their parents. What they've done too often is make a false idol out of their children, or out of their own love for them.

As a good dad, you'll want to know how to avoid that, so I want you to listen and not be too shocked when I tell you that it has nothing to do with your relationship with your children. It lies in your relationship with Me.

Come a little closer. Get to know the Source of love a little better. Allow Me to open you to your full potential. The more you know about real love, the better equipped you will be to use it for the benefit of those who are most important to you.

Don't roll your eyes at Me—and don't be the one other people roll their eyes at. Come and let Me teach you how to really love.

———————◆◆———————

*Lord, I am a comparative beginner at this parenting game.
My skills are as nothing compared with Your love. So I lay myself
at Your feet. Teach me what I need to know. Amen.*

LOOK TO YOUR COMPANIONS

When the Pharisees saw this, they asked his disciples,
"Why does your teacher eat with tax collectors and sinners?"
MATTHEW 9:11 NIV

———◆◆———

P arents can be particular about the kids their children play with. Now
you know I was never fussy about whom I hung out with, but I had a
purpose in mind.

My Father looked at My friends with a point of view very different
from the one you use when looking at your children's friends. You are
worried about your child's safety, but My Dad was worried about the
"bad" kids' eternal resting place.

Now, I'm not suggesting you let your children play with just anyone.
But I am suggesting that you set an example by looking at the guys *you*
hang out with.

God-fearing? Sure, some of them may be. The others are either
treading water spiritually or actively dragging you down. If you are
hanging out with them because that's just what you do, then you are
wasting an opportunity. Be a force for change in those lives you can
influence, and leave the ones you can't help to Me.

Show your children it doesn't matter who you hang around with
as much as it matters that you aren't just hanging around.

———◆◆———

Lord, if I would have You in my life, I must also have You in my
friendships. That might involve some changes. Give me wisdom and
compassion for those decisions, which I hope will make all my earthly
friendships a good example for my children to follow. Amen.

AT HOME IN PRAYER

Give my greetings to the brothers and sisters at Laodicea,
and to Nympha and the church in her house.
Colossians 4:15 niv

———————◆◆◆———————

Taking the time for regular family prayer time is a wonderful thing. But if you have to *make* it work, then it might be a little counterproductive.

Families who set aside time to pray together and talk about their experiences with the Father are a delight to Me. But this happens less and less as the pace of life increases and the world offers up more and more distractions.

So, what to do? Hold on to a practice perhaps better suited to another time? Give up completely and just "go with the flow"?

Neither. Give family prayer times a try, but be flexible and creative. Have these times in interesting and unusual places. Make allowances for busy lives. But let your family know that time with the Father is important—to you and to Me.

If you can imbue that time with the wonder and love it ought to have, then your children will find their own versions of it further on down the roads of their lives.

———————◆◆◆———————

Lord, if I would be a godly man, I should seek to know Your will.
If I would have a godly family, I should encourage my children to
do the same. I would have those things, and I ask Your wisdom
and help in bringing it about. May this prayer be one of many
You hear from my family, wherever they might be. Amen.

SCHOOL'S NOT OUT

I keep asking that the God of our Lord Jesus Christ, the glorious Father, may give you the Spirit of wisdom and revelation, so that you may know him better.
EPHESIANS 1:17 NIV

———————◆———————

Apart from the days you should have been there but weren't, you spent a lot of days and years at school. Why was that?

Okay, there was a lot to learn. But there was also a lot of growing to do as well. Most often, the things you took from your last classes you couldn't have learned in your first class.

Remember that it's important for you as one of your children's teachers. Your children will understand different lessons at different times, and you need to work within that timetable. And if they "forget" stuff you taught them before, don't get annoyed at them. Consider that you might have taught that lesson too soon, and then teach it again at the right time.

This is why God's people so often didn't get His meaning—and why the revelation of His work, which culminated in Me, was an ongoing process.

Lessons for life, and the hereafter, will be a progressive learning curve for your children—as they are for you.

———————◆———————

Time and again, Lord, I acquire new meaning in scripture that I had never received before. You reveal Your truths when You deem me ready to receive them. I know You will do the same for my family. May I be as patient with their growing understanding as You are with mine. Amen.

HOW IT SHOULD BE IN THE END

I press on to reach the end of the race and receive the heavenly prize for which God, through Christ Jesus, is calling us.
PHILIPPIANS 3:14 NLT

L et me end this book with a look at the present and a nod to the future.

Fatherhood is supposed to be a wonderful thing. You'll probably say it is, and in lots of different ways. But mixed in with all the wonderful stuff are problems, responsibilities, and mistakes—and being a dad would be easier without them.

Life's like that in general. It's supposed to be a great experience, but there are trials and temptations that take the shine off the whole affair.

Let Me tell you, being a grandfather is everything you thought being a father would be, and more. And heaven is everything you ever wished life could be, and then some.

In the two early stages, there's a lot of potential but a lot to be learned. In the two latter stages, well, you've earned the right to enjoy the experiences the way they ought to be enjoyed.

The Father doesn't give you all those problems and trials for no reason. And there's always a reward further down the road for those who overcome them.

Lord, I am reassured that You have my life in hand. I pray only that the lessons I learn about Your love and pass on to my children will continue to echo down through the generations. In the name of Jesus Christ my Savior, amen.

David McLaughlan used to write whatever turned a buck, but now he writes about faith and God. It doesn't pay as well—but it does make his heart sing! He lives in bonnie Scotland with Julie and a whole "clan" of children.